AF447328

FEAR

DRIVEN

SPEECH

Delete Fear and Deliver Excellence with Power and Authority

From the mind of a Former Commandant of the Airman Leadership School

MSgt Lonnie "Wade" Carter, USAF, (Ret.)

FEAR DRIVEN SPEECH

Copyright © 2022 by Wade Carter

All rights reserved. Printed in the United States of America. No part of this book may be used or reproduced in any manner whatsoever without written permission except in the case of brief quotations embodied in critical articles or reviews.

For information, visit:

http://www.MyPremierTraining.com/

First Edition: November 2022

Contents

A c k n o w l e d g m e n t s

This book is dedicated to the Airman of the United States Air Force.

Special thanks to my Lord and Savior, Jesus Christ (my life has been eternally enhanced by his spirit, blessings, and presence).

To my wife Linda, my daughters Toni, and Adriel, thank you for loving me, sticking with me when times were hard, and believing in me even when I didn't. I wouldn't be who I am today without you and your prayers. I am blessed to have you.

Grateful acknowledgments and deep appreciation are due to all the people who helped me throughout my Air Force career (my supervisors, peers, Chiefs, Commanders, fellow instructors, Instructor Supervisors, and especially my students). My students, in some cases, have done more for me than they will ever know.

Extra special thanks to my ALS Team. We shared some of the toughest and most rewarding times together. I learned so much from you, and I hope that you learned from me as well. You'll always have a place in my heart, "Post."

There are too many Air Force and sister service members who had an impact on me and who helped create the environment for me to formulate the contents of this book. Some made an impact directly, and others made an impact indirectly. I just want to be sure and say thank you to all those I served with and who've served our country. I am forever grateful to you all.

Thank you to the Community College of the Air Force (CCAF) and the hiring officials who gave me a chance to serve as a CCAF Instructor and as the Commandant of the Airman Leadership School.

Introduction

What it all means

This book was written outside the box and follows a totally different format than other speech delivery modules, books, and/or training materials. Quite honestly, this may be most impactful to the those who don't just stand and deliver speeches, but the ones who teach for a living. It is a product of my life and experience with public speaking over my 20-year United States Air Force career and will enhance instructor performance no matter what the curriculum. At the same time, life presents speaking opportunities all the time and that's what this book is all about.

The focus here is beyond the normal details in life and public speaking to the root of the issue, *fear*. Fear has a devastating effect on the individual speaker. One can do a quick internet search and find dozens of public speaking articles or "tips for public speakers". That's not what this book is about. Primarily, it deals with a new perspective on what fear is, the major areas of your public speaking performance that are impacted by fear, and what you can do about it. Specifically, it covers how fear masks your personality, steals your power and authority, as well as what mindset and behaviors you can establish that will preserve your power for *your* use.

In these pages you will receive the information and knowledge needed. *You* will have to put in the work to do what it suggests, claim victory over fear, and begin to deliver superior speech performances and improve your overall presence *anytime anywhere*.

The aim here is to arm you with the tools necessary and the motivation to be eager for your next presentation to deliver it in a way that you will be proud of. As a result, I want you to be able to stand confidently in your power and deliver masterful presentations whatever their content.

This book and the concepts/principles inside are the direct result of my leaning forward, many prayers, and years of hard work throughout my Air Force career. I had no idea that this would be the result, however, I am proud to have put this together for your benefit.

This book is delivered in 3 parts:

Part I is my story starting defeated, filled with fighting and endurance, and ending in triumph over the fear of public speaking. It follows my Air Force career, culminating in performing the duties of Commandant, Airman Leadership School (ALS) where I did all I could to give back and arm the next generation of leaders with all that

I had learned.

Part II is the result of my experience with fear, my prayers, and my observations of how fear operates and affects the public speaker. I will share with you the realizations that I had as all things fear, and public speaking came together while serving as Commandant, ALS and observing, coaching, and grading over 1600 speeches given by my students and through one breakthrough concept I heard in a sermon by Charles Spurgeon.

Part III is what I call Golden Nuggets. I recommend these golden nuggets to any instructor, speaker, supervisor, leader, manager, etc. who has mastered fear and wants to elevate their overall performance to new heights and truly stand in their power and authority. These recommendations come from my experiences and growth as an instructor in my over 3000 teaching hours and refined during my time serving as Commandant of ALS. That's really when all things came together through observing/coaching students in public speaking and self-reflection.

Part I Military Public Speaking Journey

Chapter 1 OKC to ALS

Fear
1990 to 2003
English Class

I sat in the third seat from the left four rows back in the middle of the classroom. There were 26 of us students in Mrs. Coole's English class. We were reading one of those classic literature stories they make you read through in school. We were going around the room, each student reading a few paragraphs. Cheryl, three seats in front of me, began to read, and I got lost in nervousness. Her voice became a distant mumble as I became concerned about my turn to read. Suddenly, Joe, two seats in front of me started to read and my heart started to pound. I was instantly taken away to a distant place of thunder and lightning where fear and dread began to swell. My body was tense, and anxiety filled me uncontrollably.

I wanted to run and escape to a safe place. Then, I heard Susan's voice right in front of me, and I realized my time had come. I was a moment away from suffering disgrace in front of my class. I didn't read well. I knew this wasn't going to go well. I knew I would be mocked for days after my turn to read.

When Susan stopped reading, Mrs. Coole worked to get my attention. I had no clue what was going on in the story because **my** fear in this moment had torn me away from reality. As I traveled back to reality, I found that I didn't know what paragraph we were on. I wasn't even on the right page. After being directed to the correct paragraph, my voice cracked, and my mouth dried up. It was the beginning of my utter humiliation. All eyes were on me. All ears were listening attentively, and the delay in starting to read only amplified the effects of **my** fear.

Needless, to say my reading was laughable and filled with mistakes awkward pauses. That reading and many other moments in school were exactly alike.

Roots

I am originally from Oklahoma City, Oklahoma. When I was young, my family and I moved over 15 times, and I attended ten different schools. Growing up, I was withdrawn partly because of all the moving and dealing with adjusting to so many different schools and neighborhoods. For the most part, I was still shy and withdrawn even when I joined the Air Force. Very seldomly did I ever initiate conversations with anyone except close friends or family unless I had no choice. This problem didn't change until I was well into my Air Force career.

Joining the Air Force

I was 20 years old when I entered the Air Force's delayed enlistment program. Three months later I departed home for Basic Training at Lackland Air Force Base in San Antonio, Texas. That move changed my life forever.

In Basic Training I laid low to prevent the Training Instructors from noticing me. I wasn't trying to make friends, I did what I was told, and didn't draw attention to myself. I was so withdrawn that during the second week of basic training, I went three days without saying a word to anyone. The other members of my basic training flight became concerned about my behavior and informed our Training Instructor, who was *not* happy to hear the news! For all he knew, I was a minute away from suicide or something worse. At least, that's the way it seemed when he called me into his office and demanded that I tell him what was going on. It was rather embarrassing that my instructor had an *emergency* on my account. I truly was enjoying not talking to anyone, but I had to break the silence to tell him what was going on. My instructor made it clear that I *must* start talking again. I explained that I understood that it must have made the others nervous, not knowing what was going on with me.

After all, we spent every minute of the day together.

I completed Basic Training and then Technical Training at Fort Leonard Wood, Missouri (Vehicle Operations Apprentice Course) and returned to Lackland AFB which turned out to be my first duty assignment.

At the beginning of my third year of enlistment and shortly before a deployment, I made up my mind that I was going to reenlist and stay in the Air Force until retirement.

Involuntary Baptism into Public Speaking

I had gone undetected most of my life, not putting myself out there in public. All that changed when I deployed to France. On that deployment, part of my job was to brief new incoming personnel (about three times a week) on French driving conditions, safety, and rental car procedures for the local area. This was the first time I had to deliver a presentation in front of a large group of people, and it was unavoidable.

The newcomer's briefing was just like hundreds of other briefings I have witnessed in my time in the military. There were several topics, each briefed by a different subject matter expert (SME). I happened to be the sixth in line to address the audience. I was not an SME on my topic as I had only just arrived in France myself. Nevertheless, it was my job to do the briefing and so, there I was going through a swirling mental, physical, and spiritual transformation while waiting for my turn to brief. This was ten-fold the intensity of reading out loud in school.

I gave my portion of that newcomer's briefing on a grand total of four occasions! My Unit Commander and Chaplin pulled me aside after each time and counseled me on what I could and could not say during the brief. I had been spouting off things during the brief that didn't fit the topic and even making statements that were completely inappropriate in any professional setting. My nerves were so bad that I had no knowledge of some of the things I had said or done during those sessions.

I *can* still remember, however, the feeling of fear gripping me as I watched the other presenters. I feared for them, then as each person finished their portion of the brief, I feared for me! When it was my turn, I nearly blacked out. I walked around the presenter's table and stepped out in the front of the room. I might as well have been walking out on a diving board over the mouth of a volcano. I stared at the slides instead of looking at the audience. I tried to read which of course I was unsuccessful at and by default, terrible at best. The sensations that came over my body created such intense heat that I became instantly dehydrated. My arms and legs went from normal, to tingling, to numb and then back again. My mouth dried up like a creek bed during a drought. It was so bad that I couldn't speak as my tongue stuck to the roof of my mouth. It was miserable. I noticed every error during the briefing and that magnified the intensity of the entire situation. I was a complete joke, and to say I was embarrassed would be putting it lightly. Mortified more accurately describes the feeling.

After the fourth time I performed the newcomer's brief, my Unit Commander forced my supervisor to conduct the briefing for the remainder of the deployment. I was ashamed, as well as ecstatic! My supervisor didn't enjoy doing his subordinate's job, but he understood the situation for what it was. There was no way to fix **my** problem during that short 3-month tour with all the other duties that he was responsible for.

Romance

During that tour, I paid the airfare for my girlfriend to come to France for a week. I realized at the time that if I didn't propose to her, she had planned to propose to me. So, I set up this make-believe trip to take her on. We left the hotel and while we were out driving around, I had arranged for the hotel chef to set up a romantic dinner for two in my room. When I felt enough time had gone by, I told her I had forgotten something at the hotel and needed to drive back.

We arrived and I convinced her to come up to the room with me. She was surprised. We had a great romantic meal, and then I presented the engagement ring, asked her to marry me, and she said yes!

Joy and Pain

After returning from the deployment to France, I was eligible for promotion to Staff Sergeant and the transition to Non-Commissioned Officer (NCO). I studied hard for the promotion test. I tested and beat the promotion cutoff for Staff Sergeant by 6 points. Then, I realized what I had done! Because I earned the promotion, I would now be required to attend the Airman Leadership School (ALS), and *everyone* knew what that meant. ALS required students to perform a total of *five* graded speeches! Not until after ALS graduation would I become an NCO.

I knew from my public speaking experience on my deployment to France that I was *no good* for those speeches! However, I was working to know God, reading my bible, and praying a lot. So, knowing the little that I knew then, I encouraged myself in the Lord, prayed about it, and went to

ALS with the intention of blowing those speeches out of the water!

On the first day of ALS, the time came for the students to go around the room and introduce themselves, and the instructor asked each of us, "What do you expect to get out of ALS?" Then, my turn came, and I spoke with confidence. I declared that I would beat **my** stage fright and have *five* amazing speeches. It felt so good to make that announcement, and it felt even better when I received encouragement from some of my classmates, but that faded quickly on the day I was to deliver that first speech.

That first speech was formatted to be the easiest speech of the five, and the goal was to deliver a short speech about nothing but what you already know. This is supposed to eliminate the problem of not knowing your subject and make starting the public speaking portion of the curriculum simple for everyone. "Just talk about you and your Air Force job." Sounds easy but let me tell you, I messed that up.

The instructor let the students determine our firing order (the order we would like to give our speeches). I was number 8 of 15 students in the firing order. As I watched my classmates perform their speeches, my nerves began to rise like the morning sun. I grew more nervous during each of my classmates' speeches. I was nervous for them and nervous for me. Different levels of nervousness came on me like bands of a hurricane around the eye of the storm. My nerves were amplified more than ever before. Nonetheless, when it was my turn, I said a small prayer and headed to the front of the classroom to perform my *well-rehearsed* speech. I was soaring with confidence as I looked around the room gazing into the eyes of each one of my classmates. The instructor gave the go-ahead nod, and I acknowledged it with a nod of my own.

I glanced at my speech outline to be sure I started my introduction *as planned,* and when I looked up again…I froze. My mind went blank. The spirit of fear took over my whole body, and it stiffened. My temperature rose, I nearly blacked out, and I could not remember anything that I had prepared. I looked around the room again and could hardly breathe. Just seconds ago, I looked around and I swear it made more excited, but now! The floor might as well have suddenly fallen out from under me. I stood there silently for what felt like an hour but was probably right at 45 seconds. That's when I opened my mouth, "Excuse me," I said as I picked up my speech outline and scampered out the door and down the hall. That was enough for me. I felt like I had just escaped death, and my instructor was the commander of my own personal firing squad.

I ended up in the student breakroom at the end of the hallway, and a few seconds later, a classmate came down the hall, found me and asked, "Are you coming back?" I said, "NO!" Then, he turned and went back to the classroom. A minute or two later, another classmate came down the hallway to tell me that the instructor had decided to let all the other students perform their speeches and that I would be last. I responded, "I don't care!"

When all the other speeches were completed, another classmate came to get me. "I'm not going," I said before he could talk, and he returned to the classroom. That's when the instructor came to speak with me. I told her I wasn't going to do the speech, and she told me, "Airman Carter, if you don't do your speech, you won't be allowed to graduate ALS, and you won't be able to promote to Staff Sergeant." I didn't want to lose the stripe that I had worked so hard to earn, so I explained to my instructor, who was extremely disturbed by my behavior, that I had some information in the opening (attention step) of my speech that I wasn't comfortable with, and I wasn't going to use it. I explained I'd skip that part and just introduce myself and press on with the rest of the speech. She said, "I don't care what you do. If you don't get in there and do your speech, you won't graduate, and you *won't* get your stripe."

We proceeded back to the classroom, and I placed my speech outline on the podium and waited about ten seconds for the instructor to be seated in the back of the room. She nodded, and I introduced myself, acknowledging that she had started the stopwatch. That speech was supposed to be 3 to 5 minutes long and about what I do in the Air Force. It was to have an opening attention step (which I skipped), an introduction, three main points (MPs), each with at least two subpoints (SPs), a summary, and a conclusion with transitions between each MP. I began my speech. I can't say for sure, but I believe I was in the middle of MP 2 when I busted the 5-minute mark and then in the middle of MP 3 when the instructor stopped me to move on with the day. She waved me off at around 9 minutes.

I learned something about myself from that experience. I could talk! I talked so long that the instructor had to stop me! Wow!

I then met with the instructor to receive my feedback and score after she had finished grading my performance. I was nervous about failing the speech. I don't remember anything the instructor said to me about my performance. I just know that somehow, I passed! Barely, but I passed! What a relief and encouragement!

I went on to complete and pass the remaining four speeches as well as graduate ALS and finally sewing on that Staff Sergeant Stripe. Hallelujah! Thank you, Jesus!

Chapter 2 ALS to NCOA

United States Airman
2003 to 2006
Fighting Strategically

I didn't like that I was so afraid of public speaking. I never wanted to feel that feeling again. After ALS, I found myself seeking every opportunity to get in front of an audience. I read award citations at quarterly Commander's Calls, gave safety briefings for long weekends and holidays, volunteered to facilitate meetings, and even conducted training on subjects that no one else would take, such as suicide awareness and others.

When I hit six years on active duty, I had been married for two years and had a 1-year-old daughter; I received Permanent Chance of Station (PCS) orders to Fairchild AFB, Washington where I would become the Vehicle Operations, Non-Commissioned Officer in Charge (NCOIC) for the Air Force Survival School's support squadron.

Speech Class

One of the first things I did after getting settled in at Fairchild AFB was to enroll in college at the new location. I wanted to complete my associate degree in transportation management, and to fulfill my degree, I needed to complete the General Education requirements which included speech class.

Completing that Introduction to Speech class was incredibly motivating for me. I was finally in a place where I could practice my presentation skills, work on **my** fear, and learn to put together more than just an ALS speech, which was the focus of the whole thing. That class is where I first heard of the impromptu speech. We played a game regularly in speech class. We earned extra credit toward our grade in the class by going to the back of the room and grabbing a folded piece of paper out of a topic hat and then getting in line to do an impromptu speech on that topic. The teacher couldn't keep me away from the topic hat. I must have delivered more impromptu speeches in that class than all my classmates combined.

The other students would grab a topic and sit down with it to think about what they would say about the topic. Then, they would get in line to be next. After their impromptu, they would sit back in their seats with a sense of accomplishment and relief. I'd grab a topic and get in line straight away. After each impromptu, I'd immediately grab another topic and get back in line. I wanted to gain the most out of that class, and I believe I truly did. During that class, I grew tremendously.

Promotion

I approached promotion the same way that I approached stage fright. I wasn't ready to be a Technical Sergeant, but I knew that I could do it. I just needed to get there. When I became eligible for testing, I studied for months like I was in college, took the tests, and after waiting for the results, I learned I made Technical Sergeant and beat the cutoff by 12 points!

I was not just working on getting promoted. I wanted to defeat that fear. I wanted to be confident. I wanted to know that I was good at public speaking because fear has a silent presence that can paralyze you subconsciously. It wasn't until I was already in the blazing fire in front of the audience that I'd realize I was burning and how badly. By then it's too late.

When I found out that I had scored high enough to get promoted to Technical Sergeant, I immediately started requesting a seat in the next available Non-Commissioned Officer Academy (NCOA). At the NCOA, I would get to experience the next level of leadership and management training following ALS and even more speeches! I was more than eager to attend. I even applied to be an NCOA Instructor. I thought if I could work daily in front of an audience, I'd not only defeat **my** fear of public speaking, but I'd also grow with the curriculum as a leader and manager. I wanted to teach because it would give me the best chance at ditching **my** loser friend (fear).

National Prayer Breakfast

During that time, I lived in base housing, my wife and I had become good friends with our neighbors Ethan and Erica. Ethan was the catholic administrator at the base chapel, and Erica was a Chaplain's Assistant. Ethan and I frequently talked about God and theology, among other things. One day Ethan asked me if I'd be interested in saying the prayer for the National Prayer Breakfast event at the Base Chapel. I thought, "If God set this up, who am I to turn it down?" I agreed, and a few days later, he sent me an email with the prayer breakfast's agenda and the prayer that I was supposed to read.

Woah! I thought I was going to pray like I always do

naturally, pray whatever comes to mind. I didn't know that the prayer would be pre-written. "Oh, this wasn't good," I thought. First, I don't read well publicly. Now this was even worse because I was to represent God for this prewritten public prayer reading. I had gotten myself into a mess that I did not want to be in. However, I reminded myself that I could not say no if God had set this up. So, for two days, I practiced reading that prayer. The national prayer breakfast came, I read the prayer, and I don't remember anything else about it. I was so overly stressed out and full of anxiety that the only memory I had of it was a video captured of me reading that prayer. It was embarrassing to watch. Not only do I not read well in public, but I had recently shaved my head and had a big cut on my eyebrow from an incident prior to the prayer breakfast. I looked terrible, and in my opinion the reading wasn't good. I told myself, "I did all I could to represent God at that moment and that's what matters."

Many times, over the years, I have been asked to bless the food at a potluck dinner or deliver the invocation at a ceremony, and I've always gone back to that same idea; if God set this up, who am I to say no? You could use that as a method for any public speaking invites. After all, isn't it natural when the circumstances point to you as to anyone else? Due to your position, your boss asks you to do a presentation. "Who am I to say no? Who am I to resist this opportunity? The average Mindset about the "opportunity" is incorrect and flawed because it isn't seen as an opportunity. It is seen as a threat or burden.

New Opportunity

While waiting for an opportunity to attend the Academy I received an email stating that my career field's technical training school, the Vehicle Operations Apprentice Course at Fort Leonard Wood, Missouri, was looking for instructors as they were increasing their instructor numbers by nine. After talking with my wife and considering all things, I decided to apply for the instructor job at Fort Leonard Wood. One of the smartest things about this decision for me was that I had already been through the course and had years of experience in the career field. Consider me the SME!

Shortly after I applied, I was hired, and at about that same time my wife and I had our second daughter! I was going to take my growing family with me to Fort Leonard Wood, Missouri, and become the Air Force's newest Vehicle Operations Apprentice Course Instructor. But first, I was notified that my request to attend the NCO Academy had been granted.

Just like ALS, the NCO Academy consisted of 6-weeks of leadership and management training. However, this time it only included three speeches. I put a ton of passion and effort into completing the course *and* those speeches. After one of those speeches, my instructor told me, "Sergeant Carter, you have a lot of passion. You just need to find the right platform."

Chapter 3 NCOA to Combat Comm

Hard Lessons 2006 to 2009
Professional Training

When I first arrived at Fort Leonard Wood, I was excited about being an Instructor at the Vehicle Operations Apprentice Course. I bought a house and got my family settled just in time to attend the 6-week Air Force Basic Instructor Course (BIC) at Sheppard AFB, Wichita Falls, Texas.

The course was set up like so. We had to select various topics and create lesson plans, then deliver them to the class at progressively longer lesson delivery times. I believe I had five lessons to complete: a 5-minute, a 15-minute, a 35-minute, and a 50-minute lesson. The fifth and final lesson was also a 50-minute lesson, but this one had to be an official lesson from the Vehicle Operations schoolhouse. My personal lesson topics were all survival-related: 5-minute fire craft, 15-minute survival food (insects), 35-minute knot tying, and 50-minute shelter building. For my 50-minute schoolhouse lesson I chose a lesson on Global Positioning System (GPS).

During the instructor course, I realized I was in over my head. While my lessons all passed the evaluation of my instructor, several of my classmates seemed to have been teaching for years. They were great! My lessons had good content, and the class did learn a few things from my presentations. However, my overall stage presence was severely lacking. I didn't have what those guys had, and I had no idea how to get it or even what it was. Nonetheless, I'd head back to Fort Leonard Wood to become a better instructor and prove that fear had nothing on me. It would be smart to acknowledge that this was the first time since my strategic fight against fear that I was no longer just trying to get better, but I was finally able to compare myself to others. It had taken me 4 years and 9 months to get to this point in my progress. It must be time to work on improving my overall performance.

Instructor Duty

After graduating BIC and returning to Fort Leonard Wood, I was finally going to pick up my first class of 15 students and push them through our 6-week Vehicle Operator/Dispatcher curriculum. I had ideas of how great I was going to be. I had visions of my success right after graduating the instructor course, after all, I had earned my instructor badge. I was so excited that I even went to Military Clothing Sales and bought a Master Instructor badge which had a heavy requirement of teaching hours and other requirements involved to earn it. I had plans to master teaching and reach the highest achievements as an instructor.

My first three weeks of teaching were a complete disaster! I must have been the worst instructor those students ever had, even to this day. I made every mistake that I had learned about in BIC, ALS, NCOA, speech class, or had ever heard of. Not to mention, the course was moving so fast that I couldn't keep up! I didn't have the capability nor the energy to read through and master the material overnight and deliver a full day's worth of instruction the next day. I thought for sure I was going to be fired any minute. Then it happened!

In the fourth week of training, the day came to deliver the GPS lesson which I had performed at BIC. I had no idea what a difference it would make. I taught that lesson like I had been teaching it for 20 years. It was great, fantastic, brilliant! Well, compared to the last three weeks' worth of lessons anyway. The rest of the course went well after teaching that GPS lesson. I grew in confidence, but I still needed a major rescue before I would ever be considered a good instructor.

Areas in which I was lacking were lesson delivery, stage presence, questioning techniques, subject mastery, emphasis on voice, eye contact, audience involvement, use of space, etc. Basically, if there was anything that improves a speaker's/teacher's quality, I needed it.

After my first class graduated, I was relieved (1) because my students had graduated and gone and (2) because I wouldn't have to be the lead instructor for a class again for roughly nine weeks. Then, I'd pick up my second class. In the meantime, I would assist the other instructors with their lessons, as multiple instructors were required and of course, I'd have time to rehearse my own lesson delivery skills and continue to study the curriculum to keep it fresh.

The weekend went by after my first class graduated and on Monday morning, Master Sergeant Saunders (my instructor supervisor) pulled me into his office and informed me that by teaching through that six weeks I had qualified as an instructor and could now teach without another instructor evaluating me in each lesson. However, my performance was less than desirable, so he made the call to put me back in the class rotation as soon as possible to keep things fresh for me. He informed me that I'd be picking up my second class in ten days.

Oh, my goodness! I felt like I had spent 6 weeks fighting with a heavyweight champion and barely survived and just having been released from the emergency room; my promoter had signed me up for a rematch for the title! I needed a vacation, not a new class start date!

Round Two

I was so afraid to repeat those first three weeks again that, in a move of desperation, I went to Technical Sergeant Baker, who was getting ready to start the next class, and asked him if I could sit in the back of his classroom and watch him teach the first week of the course to get myself ready for my next class. He agreed, and I sat in on his class, hoping helplessly to gain confidence, more knowledge of the curriculum, herculean instructor strength, and maybe some stamina.

During that week, I was completely shocked at what I saw that man do in the classroom! I observed so many purposed blunders, mispronounced words, jokes (some inappropriate), outrageous claims, stories, name-calling, strange explanations, etc. I couldn't believe what I was witnessing. The lessons I taught had been professional, on-topic, relevant, and… boring, underprepared, shameful flops! I was amazed at how this man was able to keep his students engaged with the curriculum and have them laughing, commenting, and interacting not only with him but also with their classmates. This was week one! He had achieved in a few days what I never saw in 6 weeks with my first class. I was both amazed and completely disappointed in myself.

When that week was over, I had only a few days before my second class started, and I had to figure out what it was that made his lessons such a big success and how I was going to get mine there. I decided to throw out all my own presumptions about professionalism, military bearing, respect for others, etc. and find who I was and how I was going to be funny and entertaining because that's what Sergeant Baker did. I had been so blinded by my own ideal of how an instructor should behave that I was the only person who didn't think Sergeant Baker was an interesting, engaging, intelligent, entertaining, great instructor.

I performed much better teaching my second class. In those six weeks, I achieved some major adjustments because of sitting through Sergeant Baker's first week of training and convincing myself that my fearful ideas weren't helping me perform. I settled down and taught one lesson at a time, got to know my students, and started *getting to know myself* in the classroom.

Sometime after that, I took three weeks off to rest and spend quality time with my family. It was great to be home and not to work full-speed teaching students while trying to master the curriculum and lesson delivery.

During the second week of leave from work, I started questioning whether I wanted to stay on active duty any longer. After all, the daily instructor duties were extremely exhausting and always challenging, at least, they were for me. I didn't want to shave my face for work anymore anyways.

During the 3rd week, and without telling anyone, I had basically made the decision to get out of the military as my 10-year mark was fast approaching and I could simply not reenlist at that point, and I'd be a civilian again. I prayed about it and asked God to show me what I should do and told Him I'd just go with whatever He says.

God Moment

My beard had always grown fast, so I developed the habit of using hair clippers to trim my beard the last day of leave before going back to work and then shaving with a razor the morning that I returned to work. It is the best way to get a clean shave without damaging my face the morning of. This time, as I was trimming my beard, I heard these words in my head. God spoke to me and said, "Now you are getting ready to do what you were meant to do." That moment changed me. I have never been the same since. I had been resisting being fully engaged in my Air Force career up to that point. Not anymore! I was no longer concerned about shaving after that!

I taught the Vehicle Operations course for three years and worked with over a thousand students. By the time I completed my tour as an Instructor, I had grown comfortable with who I am, learned how I prefer to be funny, and truly honed my ability to educate my students. I had grown in such a way that I wouldn't know until I was no longer an instructor working in the teaching environment.

Wartime Service

While performing the duties of a tech school instructor, I received orders for a deployment to Iraq to support an army special forces unit as the NCOIC of Ground Transportation for night operations on the airstrip. I had to complete two training courses in route, Anti-Terrorism Evasive Driving and Combat Skills Training. I proved to be excellent at both.

I thoroughly enjoyed my Iraq deployment. I loved supporting the special forces, doing convoy duty to deliver personnel and goods to different areas in Iraq. I loved working the airstrip and being a part of the bigger job that we had to do in the country. I truly loved working with the army and being able to experience real-world joint operations. Because of my personal efforts, advances in public speaking, and becoming a decent instructor, I found that I was also a much-improved NCO and leader in this overseas combat environment. My subordinates received me and respected me much more with my interpersonal skills developed as they were.

Stateside News

I received notice from the American Red Cross that my mother back home in Oklahoma was diagnosed with terminal cancer and that she may only have six months to two years to live.

I left Iraq earlier than originally planned given the circumstances. The Army Special Operations unit took great care of me throughout the process of sending me home. After arriving at Fort Leonard Wood, I applied for a humanitarian reassignment to Tinker Air Force Base, Oklahoma, and was approved for that transfer. My new assignment was to be the NCOIC of vehicle operations in support of the combat communications unit there.

Even though I had aspirations of great achievements as an instructor, I never did meet the requirements and earn the right to wear that Master Instructor badge before leaving the schoolhouse, though I did get close.

Chapter 4 Combat Comm to ALS Commandant

Putting it all together 2009 - 2017
Champion

While at Tinker AFB, Oklahoma, I oversaw the Combat Communications Support Squadron's Vehicle Operations Section. Because the unit was a Combat Communications unit, all support personnel had to complete the unit's Combat Skills Course. After doing so, I was selected to become a member of the support cadre for the course. However, my position as NCOIC was my primary role and ultimately took precedence.

A year later, our Group Commander made a decision that would place all the responsibility on me and my Vehicle Operations team to train over 600 personnel on 4 military vehicles (M-series): the 2.5 ton (deuce and a half), the 5 Ton Truck, the water buffalo (water distribution tank/trailer), and M-200 trailer that is meant to carry generators and other equipment.

This was the second moment in time that I recognized how much my personal excellence had increased since I worked so hard to defeat fear and, after that, refine my stage presence.

I spent two weeks developing the training lesson plans and course material, goals, and expectations. My team and I trained and certified 14 trainers bringing our qualified trainer count to 24. I taught the first month of students and sent them out driving with their trainers to work the kinks out of the new training course. It was fantastic! I trained all 6 of the Squadron Commanders and the Group Commander and, over the next four months, directed the training of 600-plus personnel.

All things had come together for me as a public speaker, trainer, and leader of my section. My personal race to be better than before had transformed me into a whole new person. I had new abilities and way more confidence and competence.

Super-vision

After my tenure at the Vehicle Operations Schoolhouse, I was tuned in to public speaking so well that at times I couldn't watch others present to an audience. I could see every error in their delivery, every slip-up in the content, every unorganized thought. I analyzed their stage presence, audience engagement, and on and on. I would be sick to my stomach, well, almost.

Anyway, I began tuning out when a presenter was bad, even pastors preaching the Word of God. I'd just find other things to think about. Sometimes, I'd write down feedback for the presenter. I'd find them after they were done, tell them who I was and a little of my experience, and then give them my feedback. For the most part, they were grateful, but every now and then one of them would take a blow right to their pride/ego. The point is that I couldn't handle bad presentations for a multitude of reasons.

Generally, when my unit had distinguished visitors, our Commander or his delegated representative would bring the visitor through our Vehicle Maintenance area to meet our Work center Non-Commissioned Officers in Charge (NCOICs). At the Support Squadron, we'd usually have from four to seven NCOICs present with their teams lined up by the work center. If there was a chance of rain, we'd line up in the maintenance bay.

The Commander would come by with the distinguished visitor and their entourage and introduce them to each of the NCOICs one at a time. Depending on the unit, visitors may come 3 or 4 times per year. These visits are like prophesied nightmares for most NCOICs. They know there will be a visit in the future but have no idea when nor how ugly it will be.

After one of these visits, again I was a bit sick to my stomach having watched my fellow NCOICs handle introducing themselves and their teams. As soon as our Commander and the visitors left, I called a quick meeting to discuss the introductions with the NCOICs. Again, I explained my instructor background and gave them feedback on what I had just witnessed. Then, I continued by giving them my "showcase your workplace" pointers for success. The next visitor received a different experience. The NCOICs had taken my advice, planned out what they would say and did it with confidence. (See Tips for the NCOIC or Section Chief in Chapter 9)

Promotion – Joining the SNCO Club

If you have been on active duty long enough to test for promotion, you know what it's like to follow the numbers for promotion testing. Well, I tracked and ran the numbers. I pushed the limits of my inner nerd's capabilities motivating myself using numbers and spreadsheets. I revisited the numbers frequently. I watched others' numbers. I observed the studying and testing routines of others. I concluded that approximately 75 to 80 percent of promotion-eligible active-duty members weren't putting in the effort to get their best shot at promotion. 15 to 20 percent were working steadily at studying and being ready to test, but only about 5 percent were truly maximizing all their energy, effort, and spare time outside of their work and life responsibilities.

I'll tell you what I always told my peers and my students. *No one can stop you from getting promoted except you.* You owe it to yourself to know and understand the promotion system so that you can maximize all the points you can. I assigned myself time to study as if I was taking a college class. I studied regularly. Testing is only once a year. The task is to figure out what amount of time to invest: how many days per week, how many hours, etc., create a schedule and commit to it. After that, you should be able to sleep at night knowing that you did all you could. The rest rides on your performance on test day.

This was my approach to testing for Staff Sergeant (promoted the first time), Technical Sergeant (promoted the first time), and Master Sergeant (promoted the second time). I was sure I would be promoted to Master Sergeant that first eligible testing cycle; however, I didn't perform accordingly. I missed the second test and received no test scores that year. Nevertheless, I did it all again the next year and beat the promotion cutoff by 20 points.

I was officially in the Senior Non-Commissioned Officer (SNCO) tier. I had been waiting for that moment for a year. I was nominated to serve as the treasurer on the board of the Top 3 enlisted private organization. As a member of the Top 3, I created and conducted a monthly mentoring session bringing together five SNCOs (including at least one Chief Master Sergeant) and 20 Airmen/NCOs. These sessions were about an hour long. I created the discussion topics, facilitated the flow of the dialog to make it most impactful, and after each session, I published notes from the session and sent them by email to all the NCOs and Senior NCOs in the group to share with their teams as they saw fit. I was in the SNCO Club, and this was the third time I had witnessed the amazing results that kept flowing from my efforts to defeat fear. It was like that old saying, "the gift that keeps on giving"!!!

I had known for some time that public speaking and simply having the right things to say at the right time wasn't a strength for most of the NCOs I had met in the last 14 years, although most of them were extremely good at the core functions on the job. What I realized as an SNCO, however, truly surprised me. Most of the SNCOs weren't strong public speakers either. While performing extremely well on the job, the skills of conveying the spoken word to an audience were severely lacking. I witnessed it in Staff Meetings and other settings that I hadn't been exposed to until I became an SNCO. I seriously didn't know that so many SNCOs had the same problems with public speaking that I had experienced. Somehow, I'd been oblivious before advancing to the SNCO tier. I concluded that on the job there simply wasn't a demand for excellent public speaking, and most people just avoided the task as much as they could.

Somehow I'd spent 14 years giving acknowledgement to the Senior NCOs above me out of obligation or some kind of default leadership structure admiration as if they had it all together and were most efficient at all things leadership and management. I was wrong.

This newly revealed reality was just evidence that public speaking fears run deep and don't simply go away in time. Fear *must* be confronted, work must be done to prevent the fear, and effort *must* be made to press past it into excellence no matter what level you're at in life or career.

When you master fear, grow in your power and authority, speak the necessary things and leave out the desperate things that fear makes you do to achieve in life and in business, your subordinates, peers, supervisors, family, friends, acquaintances, all start to "see" you for who you truly are and they begin to admire the new you without even identifying what it is about you that makes you different. It's because you are no longer *"driven by fear"*.

Season's End and a New Beginning

I was beginning to feel great about myself and my accomplishments when the purposeful move back to Oklahoma had come full circle and my mother was laid to rest. Shortly after that, the unit (Combat Communications Group) was notified that is was being deactivated and that all members (military and civilian) would be transferring to other units.

As the unit began preparations to shut its doors, the process for receiving orders to transfer yielded me a choice of Minot AFB, North Dakota, or Holloman AFB, New Mexico. My family and had chosen Holloman AFB, but I also applied for a special duty assignment to MacDill AFB, Tampa, Florida, in hopes that I might be honored with the opportunity to serve as Commandant, ALS.

God did bless me with the move and the Commandant job at MacDill AFB. However, once again, it involved training beforehand. I packed up my household and attended Enlisted Professional Military Education Instructor Course (EPMEIC) at Maxwell AFB, Montgomery, Alabama. During the six weeks at EPMEIC, I learned more about PME course material than I did teaching techniques or public speaking skills, although it was a great refresher. Because of my previous instructor experience, I found myself coaching and assisting the other students to graduate from the course and go on to their respective schoolhouses. Upon graduation, I was off to MacDill AFB, Florida, to settle my family and continue teaching, coaching, guiding, and mentoring. Only this time, I would not only be delivering lessons but directing the entire schoolhouse from onboarding new students to organizing and facilitating graduation ceremonies. Little did I know what I would learn about myself and the overall impact of fear and public speaking.

Eyewitness Account

During my time as the ALS Commandant, I saw first-hand, time and time again, the miss management of the details in my student's speech material. This part of public speaking is the simplest. It doesn't involve the audience and yet people make it so difficult.

In ALS, we gave our students the task of telling their

Air Force story. All we asked is that they have an introduction, overview, and three main points (MP): (MP1) what life was like before the Air Force, (MP2) what you do for your job, (MP3) career plans (reenlist or separate from the service), summary, conclusion, and transitions between each part of the speech. Each MP was to have two subpoints (SPs) and could have as many as needed after that. The goal was to tell their story in three to five minutes while being evaluated. A speech shorter than three minutes was an automatic failure. A speech that went long could pass the evaluation if it had already earned enough points for a passing score when the five-minute clock ran out.

Sticking to the format and the outline was, it seemed, one of the hardest tasks for most students to achieve. I evaluated off-topic speeches that were mostly about the student's father, mother, grandparent, or supervisor in the Air Force. Some speeches delivered one topic that took up all the time for the three MPs. Some were missing transitions. Some skipped whole parts of the speech altogether! This is one of the most obvious and most devastating impacts fear has on a presentation. It steps in and destroys the flow.

We asked the students to put together a one-page "keyword" outline for use during their evaluation. Some students brought in three pages written like a book. Some brought in one page typed in 8-point font written with no spaces full of top to bottom (these are not "keyword" outlines). It's so hard to watch a person try to read through a speech, but for some, it was a more monumental task to create a keyword outline than to see a keyword and start talking.

The anxiety behind putting together the information and rehearsing for time and accuracy is so intense for some that even the simplest standards were too challenging to follow.

In most cases where a student had these kinds of difficulties in the preparation stage of the speech, the evaluation was a wreck. The student would fail the speech, be counseled on their errors, and be given feedback on how to perform it better. Overnight they were asked to correct any issues in their outline and repeat the evaluation the next day.

I had a student once, who came in on speech day without an outline altogether. I pulled him aside and reprimanded him for not completing the work, and he explained that the instructors hadn't said that an outline was mandatory, and he didn't need an outline to perform his evaluation. He was right and I let him perform his speech without the outline. He passed his speech and brought in an outline the next day.

Familiar Territory

I had been fighting the good fight standing against the fear of public speaking for many years. In fact, not only did I teach at the Vehicle Operations Apprentice Course for three years and have over 1500 teaching hours, but I also took many college classes, and military training courses, sought out briefings, training sessions, mentoring sessions, and many other opportunities that came my way. Most of them I heard about one way or another, chased them down, and saw them to completion.

I fought hard to conquer stage fright, as well as my many other inefficiencies over the years. But it wasn't until I had been in the Air Force for 16 years and had prayed for and been blessed with the opportunity to serve as MacDill Air Force Base's ALS Commandant in Tampa, Florida, that I finally understood what I had accomplished in public speaking from the time I was a student at ALS to becoming the ALS Commandant.

When you become the teacher and must explain a concept that you know very well or train someone else in a certain skill that you have mastered, you will eventually have a breakthrough moment. The moment when you realize exactly what it is that *you* do that makes a thing work for you to precisely explain it to someone else. If you are a teacher for long enough, you'll have many moments of clarity like this.

In this case, I was witnessing what people go through during a speech. I watched and graded thousands of speeches being delivered by my ALS students. Most of them were stricken with fear, just like I was at the time I completed the course many years prior. My understanding of the stage fright issue became more and more clear as each class of students would come on board, complete the requirements of the course, and graduate.

There were some students who experienced minimal stage fright like the one that completed his speech with no outline. These students, some with little to no training, even made huge mistakes during a presentation and kept right on going with very little anxiety. However, most students had unbelievable anxiety about public speaking. Some, like me, experienced freakishly intense anxiety symptoms, and the great majority of them didn't completely overcome them. The fear is simply too much. I'm so thankful that I prayed to my lord and savior, Jesus Christ, for my problems with fear.

He delivered me!

Breakthrough Moment

Midway through my tour as the Commandant, I was approached by the base Public Affairs Office about conducting an ALS briefing during Civic Tours that they conduct around the base throughout the year. I agreed to brief base visitors, and ALS was added to the tour itinerary. I spoke with about 40 civilian leaders in all types of industries and from all over the world during these tours. One of the things that I found interesting is the audience's reaction to hearing about what we do at ALS. Most of the companies represented in my audience didn't have any type of professional development offered to their employees. They were often amazed to hear about our leadership and management training and how it continues throughout an Airman's career as they progress. Several times and from different tour groups, these leaders mentioned how they would love to have a program such as this to help their middle managers become more well-rounded and better prepared.

Most of the questions these tours had for me were about the public speaking aspect of the ALS training. They often asked dozens of questions relating to public speaking. Again, this is solid evidence that people everywhere are struggling with public speaking and are desperate for a solution.

My personal breakthrough happened during one of these tours when a young lady who was a middle manager in a department store company from San Antonio, Texas asked me what the key was to mastering public speaking. My answer wasn't even formulated yet. I hadn't had the time to sit and analyze the details to create a conclusion. Yet, within seconds, I knew the answer and began to explain. The entire audience was amazed! They could not believe what they were hearing and how true it was for each of them. The key is all about power and how most people give their power away before they even get close to their audience. I added that Golden Nugget to the ALS briefing from that day on. (see Moment of Truth in Chapter 7)

USAF Career

I completed my time in the Air Force as Commandant, CMSgt Aubert E. Dozier Airman Leadership School, MacDill AFB, Florida. My duty as ALS Commandant was like a dream. It was so long and difficult yet felt short and was most rewarding. It was the culmination of all my energy and effort to support the Air Force, provide for my family, and become the "whole person" the Air Force promotes, as well as the place where all things came together for me.

What I learned about myself as Commandant, ALS is that at my core, I am an investor in people. This book represents one of the most valuable byproducts of my Air Force career. I believe it is most valuable for anyone and that's why I am sharing it with you. This is an overall effort to defeat fear and give you your power back.

Part II Fear and Strategic Targets

Chapter 5 Introduction to Fear

His Name is Fear

I had been doing everything in my power to override the effects of fear. I was trained in the traditional higher education methods of public speaking. I knew all the tips. By the nature of my career path, I was in front of an audience every workday. I was basically staying so busy that fear couldn't keep up. **My** fear was snuffed out by sheer activity and determination.

I was just like everyone else. I had a stage fright problem, and I used traditional book knowledge and public speaking do's and don't's and practiced and used those tools daily to get past it. It was a long and hard road for me to overcome. There was no help. No special serum or potion would take it away. There was no hope for an easier solution.

I prayed about **my** fear of public speaking. Oh, how I wanted this problem to become easier or just be removed altogether. Then, I heard a sermon by Charles Spurgeon where he made a profound statement about fear. Charles explained fear in a way I had never heard before. He said fear is everywhere. Fear is like a family friend who you've invited into your home, and you take care of him. That's the way I remember it. Charles' words were much more elegant than my paraphrased attempt to repeat them.

Charles' description of fear changed me forever. Since then, I have taken charge of my own house, made it clear that fear isn't welcome, and encouraged many others to do the same.

My description of fear as I understand him now:

Fear is a freeloader

Fear stakes you out. He takes his time and covertly makes friends with you. He moves in and takes up square footage in your home. He eats your food, sleeps in your spare room or living room, and never cleans up after himself. He drains you, and somehow you don't even realize what's going on. You feel like the relationship is unbreakable (that he'll always be there). You're used to him and even comfortable with him always by your side. Everyone who sees you sees him with you, even when you don't acknowledge his presence. You tend to his needs. You make sure that he has a roof over his head and a bed to sleep in. He feeds off your willingness to keep him in your home. He affects all your relationships and makes you feel that this lifestyle is standard.

Fear Strikes at Will

From his hidden position in your home, Fear can paralyze you without notice. He affects your nervous system and all other systems simultaneously. He raises the heat, taunting you and binding you to inactivity, or else you'll embarrass yourself tremendously. When the moment has passed, and you are able to behave normally again, his *best work* is in his ability to calm you down and focus the attention on *you* and away from *him*. As a result, you go on believing you're the problem, and he continues to go undetected. You even declare, "I hate public speaking" or "I have terrible stage fright." All the blame rests with you.

Please notice where I have written the word "my" in bold a few times earlier in the book. This is a sign that a person has excepted fear into their home and claimed him as a family friend to nurture and keep him. It's evidence of his ability to put the ownership of the problem on you while *he goes on undetected.* He doesn't want you to know that he is a personality.

Truth

The truth is you don't have to keep the freeloader

around. You have rights! When will you exercise your right to act solely on your own without fear affecting how you behave? After all, it is *your* home! He doesn't pay you rent or buy you groceries. As a matter of fact, he doesn't do *anything* that benefits you. Fear limits your potential and hides the real you from your audience.

Eviction

It's time to kick him out. You must confront him in all truth. Yes, you've been together for longer than you can remember. No, you don't know how to behave on your own, and that's a bit scary because it's unknown territory, but you must do it for freedom's sake. Don't think about what it will be like when you confront him. What you can't comprehend is that the anxiety about what it will be like when you kick fear out of your house is the result of *his* influence.

Freedom

Once Fear is removed, you'll have to make a lot of adjustments to living life free on your own. You'll have to get your house back in order once Fear leaves the premises. You don't remember ever living like this before, free. This may take a good amount of time. It could take months. Don't be discouraged. Get excited! Get up and get free. Get comfortable being you. Enjoy yourself and get ready to deliver genuine, fearless, masterful speeches.

The Importance of this moment

This chapter, this new perspective, and this understanding of fear is the critical and cardinal point of this book. If you are unwilling to see this truth or unwilling to take a stand against <u>fear as a personality</u>, then hand this book to someone else who will benefit. The rest of this book is of no use to you.

There are many books on public speaking and mastering the fear of public speaking. They talk abundantly about the effects of the fear of public speaking and the physiological issues one has concerning public speaking. Some even go as far as to suggest drugs (sedatives and tranquilizers) to settle the fear. All these approaches ignore the root cause and band-aid or patch the problem so that you can "get by" and hopefully get better at public speaking.

Acknowledging fear for who he is and taking a stand for freedom will bring you to the place where you can, as all the public speaking experts say, "Be yourself," and that's because fear blocks your personality and your ability to be genuine with your audience. Fear also, blocks you from understanding who you are and keeps you from exploring what you might like. Your own interests are hidden by fear.

Resistance

When I was 16 years old, I inherited the family vehicle (a 1976 Chevy van), and one day while traveling to another town to hang out with some of my friends, the engine seized up on the highway and rendered the van useless. After having it towed home, my mother made an agreement with her brother to move the van to my grandfather's backyard until repairs could be made.

My uncle Allen showed up with his truck to tow my van back to my grandfather's house. He sat me down and briefed me on how to manage the van while he pulled it with a chain and his old ford pickup. He gave me a general understanding of the towing and towed vehicle relationship and the safety measures involved. In his guidance, he explained that when it was time to go forward, he would use his truck to pull me up to speed, and it was my job to manage the amount of slack in the chain between the two vehicles so that when it tightened, the vehicles didn't jerk hard against each other. He said everything would just flow smoothly. When it was time to stop at a red light, it was my job to use the van's brakes to slow both vehicles down until we stopped. That way, the chain would be tight the whole time.

We hooked up the chain and started down the road. I

was keeping the chain taught, he was driving and pulling us through the traffic lights, and then we entered the ramp onto the highway. I believe the speed limit was 60 miles per hour, and I was managing the slack in the chain by holding the brake pedal slightly. That was keeping the chain nice and tight, not allowing the chain to drag on the ground. Eventually, my uncle started using his brakes. This was at the time before cell phones, so we didn't have a way to communicate. He was waving his hand out the window basically trying to get me to stop. I finally pulled over on the shoulder of the highway. Then he proceeded to jump out of the truck, very upset. I could tell in his body language that he was extremely frustrated.

He approached the van, and as I was rolling the window down, he started yelling at me. "What are you doing? Are you holding the break the whole time?" I said, "Yes, I was keeping the chain taught." He was so upset. All I know is that he wanted me to stop holding the brake and just let the van be pulled, and only if the chain is extremely slack do I give it any brakes and don't hold the break the entire time. He eventually said, "I can't even get up to the speed limit. You need to let me go the speed limit." "Oh," I said. I told him I would just let him pull me, and he got back in the truck. Then, we continued the rest of the way to my grandfather's house.

I was young and inexperienced. I had never done this before, and it was dangerous. So, I had a lot of fear, and he had explained what kinds of things could happen if that chain had gotten loose enough to drag it on the ground, so I was doing everything I could to keep that chain off the ground and keep us flowing. Because of fear, I was resisting his plan. He understood the idea of how this should go. By holding my brakes, I was creating resistance and making it harder for him to do the job even though he knew how to get the job done the right way.

Resistance Mindset

What is your level of resistance to the speech? I don't need to know, but you do. It's important to understand where your commitment is to engage with the audience, and sometimes you truly need to tell yourself how to behave or to be more committed. You might tell yourself, "Get excited!" It's ok to get excited.

Most leaders and managers lose sleep over having to deliver a presentation to an audience of their senior leaders. It is too overwhelming. To have their credibility as a leader and manager hanging in the balance generally makes even the best leaders/managers cringe while building up resistance.

Here's what that resistance sounds like. I wish it was not my job to deliver this material. I have no desire to perform this speech. I don't want to organize the discussion points. I don't want to be here. I don't care about this subject. This is just part of my job and a part of my job that I do not like. I wish I didn't have to do it. Why can't they get someone else to do this?

Anytime this resistance is in your mind, it directly opposes your power and authority for delivering your speech. It dilutes it. It's like an off-duty police officer engaging with a suspect as if the officer is clearly suited up for the job with his badge in full view. Let's say the officer is in plain clothes saying, "freeze" while pointing a gun at a suspect. It's not going to produce the same reaction from the suspect because they don't know that he's a policeman. When you have resistance in your mind, it sets you up for failure just like the plain clothed policeman. Because of your resistant actions, decisions, and behaviors, your audience will not acknowledge your authority, recognize your power, nor will they know you're the SME. Why should they pay you any attention? Your resistance to the speech reduces your credibility. It makes everything confusing instead of bringing clarity, and it leads your audience to mentally check out and wait for your presentation to be over.

Get determined to accomplish your speech instead of resisting it. Let your mind be on the results of the message delivered, not the opinions of your audience. This will keep your focus right where it needs to be, on the purpose of your speech, and not listening to the lies fear wants you to believe.

Where Fear Attacks

Speeches are often like disaster films. First, some smart person picks up the clues that there is a major catastrophe about to happen. Then, the smart one starts notifying people that may be able to help eliminate the coming calamity. While these capable people start working on plans to solve the problem, fear steps in and causes confusion, disagreements, second-guessing and overall bewilderment which leads to bad decisions and plans derailing. The situation becomes so bad that fear becomes dread, and we find our main characters left stranded, hoping for a miracle.

Fear attacks covertly, causing confusion and creating gaffes. Fear can turn even the best thinkers into, "um, uh…" stallers. Fear makes good speakers subconsciously beg for confirmation that the audience is listening, "right?" Fear makes even the most confident individual fidget, clicking a pen or playing with a wedding ring. Fear brings out the most awkward laugh, used as a crutch to keep the speaker from feeling alone. Fear causes such insecurity that the speaker can't look the audience in the eyes while trying to remember MPs. The floors and ceiling get a lot of attention when this happens. Fear skips through a speech like a small child who is given a lollypop and told to go play, forcing the speaker to skip whole MPs or SPs.

To take back your power, you must be able to rid yourself of fear. You *can* do it. I know because I *did* it.

Chapter 6 Fear Targets Your Personality

Preconceived Idea of Who You Must Be

In this chapter, we're going to eliminate your desire to be who you think you should be and instill the freedom to be who you really are. For all of us, when we are asked to give a speech, we have a preconceived idea of what it should look like given the situation, the audience, and the requester. In certain situations, you might imagine that you need to be funny or professional, tell jokes or be persuasive, be entertaining, or be the knowledge expert for your audience. Truthfully, you are stressing yourself out expecting to be all those things.

While those things could be in every speech, not all of them need to be at their highest levels for everyone each time. The task is to find *your* sweet spot.

Let's not forget in Chapter 3 under Instructor Duty that, I decided to throw out all my own presumptions about professionalism, military bearing, respect for others, etc. This lead me down a path of discovery and eventually I found who I am. I discovered my own sense of humor and learned how to be funny and entertaining. I learned that when I thought something was funny, my audience began to think it's funny too. Before this, I had been so blinded by my own ideal of how an instructor should behave that I had bound myself in a prison of rules and standards that I'd never be able to live up to. There might be someone out there that can meet those requirements, but it isn't me and never would be. Letting go of those preconceived expectations I gave myself license to explore and discover who I am and what works for me. This choice amplified my ability to keep fear from interfering with my performance by attempting to tell me I wasn't good enough, I wasn't funny, my students don't like me nor respect me, etc.

Now I understand who I am. I thrive on competence, so I work hard to understand my subject and builds my confidence. I am a knowledge expert at heart. I enjoy the process of transferring knowledge, but I weave in comedy on the spot and tell stories when a story naturally fits into the flow of the speech while keeping my overall communication as accurate as possible. For me the information must be accurate. So, I am aware that I need to know that what I am saying is accurate. I am comfortable directing attention to what I observe in my audience for the occasional laugh, and stories help me highlight concepts to my audience and I don't want to give false information.

Once you understand naturally who you are, the only thing left is to get comfortable *being* you, right there in your sweet spot. No matter how many times you practice your speech, it will always sound different. **Don't be alarmed**. Watch/listen to your performance, keep what feels good to you, and get rid of what is uncomfortable or *not really you*. The goal should be not only to get familiar with the speech outline or lesson plan but to listen to yourself. Observe, don't be critical. Just observe and get comfortable in that place where that speech lives.

Discomfort

Next time you go out to a new movie in a theater. Find a decent size rock and put it in your back pocket. Watch the movie all the way through without removing that rock. This is how uncomfortable your audience is when you're not behaving naturally. Essentially, your personality is masked by fear, and everything becomes unnatural. This discomfort is first felt by you and then interpreted by your audience through many types of nervous ticks, errors, and general awkwardness. They will recognize that the whole performance feels forced or fake. There will always be something wrong and most of the time, neither you nor your audience will pinpoint exactly what it is. You need to be natural, and when you aren't, it shows.

The Environment of a Speech

So often, when we enter another person's house, we initially withdraw and observe as we slowly adjust to the environment. But if we are there for a while, then we relax and start behaving more natural. We go through a process of taking in the environment and slowly become comfortable in that place.

The person's house is different than yours. They live a different way. Their family members are different. They don't have the same pets. They don't have the same artwork or the same TV. They don't eat the same foods, and everything about their environment is foreign. So, it takes a little time to settle in and become comfortable. Communicating with them makes it easier because there's a flow taking place between you.

You take in feedback from your surroundings, reactions from the family, the pets, tasting the dinner, talking about different things like the neighborhood or how long they've lived there or what home improvement projects they have planned or have done already. After you eat together, have some drinks, and participate in activities, you become much more comfortable and feel more open to speaking naturally the way you normally do.

Understand that the person's house is the speech itself. The environment is your audience. If you are a repeat visitor to the house (speech), the environment (audience) may change each time. If there are different guests, you may return to being less comfortable. Over time, visit after visit, you will naturally become more comfortable with the variations in the environment at the person's house. This is exactly what giving a speech is like when it is repeated over and over to different audiences. **The only thing that remains the same is you.**

What if you could behave and deliver your speech in the way that you might deliver that speech after 20 visits to it? Wouldn't it be nice to visit that speech the very first time and be natural and genuine?

Find yourself right where you are. Get rid of all the preconceived notions about your speech, your audience, and expectations you've created in your own mind, and **focus on being comfortable**. Focus on what you enjoy, why you want to deliver your speech, and your purpose for the speech, and stay genuine.

Find the comedy, tell the stories, be entertaining, interesting, and accurate. Practice with your speech content until it clicks. Then, know that it is all about you and be ready to experience whatever comes out of your mouth, knowing that the speech will never be the same twice. Relax and enjoy yourself. You are home. Understand that you should be bringing the environment to the audience, not the other way around. The audience should be trying to get comfortable with the atmosphere you create just as much as you feel you need to get comfortable with them.

Now that fear is gone, you must figure out who you are

Read through this series of statements and decide if you agree or disagree. Return to this as often as needed to drill down your natural tendencies more accurately. When you truly know yourself, you will easily be able to identify nervous ticks you may have while presenting to an audience and work to eliminate them.

WARNING

You must be honest to yourself. If you are having a hard time saying I agree or disagree with a particular statement, this may be an area where you have an opinion about that statement that is hindering you from being who you are.

Example: Let's say that you don't like hippies and the

statement, in your mind, represents or depicts something distinctly hippy. Obviously, you don't want to be like a hippy. Here's where the harm lies for you.

You must be ok with and embrace having a quality that you'd associate with an idea you don't like.

If not, you'll never be free to be yourself.

I generally seek to belong.

Engaging with people drains me.

I feel the need to organize everything.

It's easy for me to visualize ideas, concepts, and principles.

I appreciate when emphasis is placed on important ideas.

I tend to question the established rules or procedures.

I am a great storyteller.

I must see a project through to completion.

I solve problems by using what I know works rather than experimentation.

I thrive on action and adventure.

I love being the center of attention.

People say I'm a great listener.

I usually compromise rather than compete.

I energetically express emotions.

I prefer visual learning.

I consider myself to be creative.

I follow trends.

I enjoy structured events.

I love making people laugh.

I am more serious than most people I know.

I avoid unnecessary confrontation.

Your tendencies will have a major impact on your speech delivery. Your goal is to identify those that boost your performance and lean on them while eliminating the others. Learn to tailor your tendencies to benefit your overall impression on the audience. Develop your speech to complement your personality. Do what you enjoy. When you enjoy your delivery, your audience will feed off that energy.

Terrible Advice

If you've read or listened to any public speaking advice in the past, then you have most likely heard the advice, "You want your style to stand out." There is a tremendous problem with that statement! It leads the speaker on a quest to conjure up some mystical aberration that separates them from *who* they *are*.

Think about this. Your fingerprint is uniquely yours, with no match anywhere else in the world. Your personality is exactly like your fingerprint. You are just as unique without following the terrible advice to try to create some kind of special effect on your audience. You are uniquely you. Your style is already there, intact somewhere inside. Fear was the only thing standing in the way of your style.

If you've thought, "I'm not good enough," or "Someone else should be giving this speech," then you need to understand that **fear is a liar**. When you're able to stand comfortably with confidence before your audience and be yourself with no tricks, then your natural style will do the work of entertaining your audience while your message is being delivered with accuracy and audience engagement.

The fear of public speaking ruled the way I presented to an audience for years and I let it happen. After my disastrous first class as a Vehicle Operations Instructor, I began to develop a rhythm. I broke loose from all preconceived ideas of what a good instructor is. I developed or better stated; I *discovered* my own style. It was breaking free from that idea of what I should be and the fear behind knowing that I couldn't achieve it that unlocked my style.

I know what you're thinking: "Style? I don't have any style". Don't worry. If you're commanding fear to leave and denying his authority to live in your home and, thus, influence you, your style will emerge on its own. **Get comfortable, and everything else will flow.**

I also discovered that I have an alternative motive that I naturally weave into everything while delivering a speech or a specific curriculum. I like to help people, and that influences my delivery. It influences when and how I emphasize certain ideas.

The knowledge of who you are has a huge impact on your stage presence. Forget about what your audience might be expecting! They don't have to give your presentation, you do! Have confidence in yourself, the all-natural, genuine you!

Things Fear Says to You

I'm quitting

I'm not the person for this

Someone else should be doing this

I'll never get it right

I'm too nervous

I'll always fail

I'd rather be anywhere but here

I don't need this

It's not worth my time and energy

I'd rather be at home doing nothing

In the sales industry, they call this head trash. I say, "Fear leads to resistance, resistance leads to hopelessness, and this is what hopelessness sounds like." – Wade Carter

Remember This

You don't have to be perfect for your audience. They will respect you for being you even if some don't like you.

I've received written or verbal feedback from over 3000 students. Some of that feedback was hard to accept, some was truly uplifting and increased my courage to keep pushing forward. All of it was useful to drive my performance to new heights. Below are some examples of feedback I have received, and it should stand as proof that you will not be perfect for everyone in your audience. Certain personalities simply will not align with yours. It's up to you to accept that, act on any useful feedback to make yourself better, and continue being genuine regardless of how it feels to hear it.

Feedback examples:

MSgt Carter - Used stories and transitions to connect the lessons. It helped a lot of us retain the content.

MSgt Carter - I enjoyed MSgt Carter's attitude and his actual care for others and his students.

MSgt Carter - Did not have much interaction like I had hoped for - your stories are awesome. Try to get to know everyone a little bit and not just a few students.

MSgt Carter - Good. Too many stories.

MSgt Carter - Motivational talks are great. Easy to talk to.

MSgt Carter - Funny and energetic. Did an amazing job keeping us engaged.

MSgt Carter - Yes, I did enjoy his stories. Seemed long-winded, but only happened a couple of times.

MSgt Carter - Awesome approach.

MSgt Carter - Very good at portraying information. Very reasonable. Great instructor.

MSgt Carter - Very motivating as in he is always

positive and conveys lessons with expertise. He helped me retain lesson info by explaining lesson concepts in a very precise and entertaining way. MSgt Carter was by far the most influential instructor and one of the top MSgts I have come across in my Air Force Career.

MSgt Carter - Yes. I still don't know what shaving your face has to with ALS or Resisting, but I remembered the moment I stopped resisting, and that made me aware that that was happening. Loved story time, and I can tell you genuinely care and take a lot of pride in what you do. Thank you.

MSgt Carter - Like his humor/motivating

MSgt Carter - Very motivating. His quirkiness caught my attention immediately, and he's able to convey lessons extremely effectively.

MSgt Carter - Very motivating, knows how to pick your brain and work towards alternate perspectives.

MSgt Carter - Emotionally intelligent and shared helpful insight attached to mentorship.

MSgt Carter - Told non-beneficial stories at inappropriate times. Never motivated me! Actually, did the complete opposite!! I wish he cared more about his students.

MSgt Carter - Stories are not very effective. The lesson only consisted of questions. Not effective.

When you get feedback, guard yourself against allowing the negative feedback a place in your heart where fear can use it to destroy your progress. Understand that even though you have commanded fear to leave and taken back your own house, he will stay close and wait for a new opportunity to get back in. He loves to exploit self-doubt. Stay encouraged. Fear doesn't control you. You control him.

Life of the party

There was a time when my family had been invited to a get-together at my wife's friend's house. This was a friend I had only briefly met, but I had not met her husband. To be honest, I didn't want to go. If you've ever been in that situation, then you know you're losing the battle of first impressions when you have this attitude. Well, I didn't want to be a disappointment, and I didn't want to give my wife's friend and her husband a bad impression. There were going to be several other families there whom I hadn't met. I didn't want to embarrass myself by not being in the mood for entertaining.

On this occasion, I spoke to myself quietly, saying, "I'm going to be the life of the party," and I meant it. When we arrived at the house, I enthusiastically introduced myself to the hosts and all the other guests. This was a typical BBQ get-together. There were about six families there. We spent time on the back deck of the house and in the backyard. Kids played games, and adults sat around a firepit having drinks, eating, and having different discussions.

I'm generally quite reserved and take in the environment for quite some time before I engage in full-length conversations. However, on this occasion, I was the conversation driver in most of the discussions. I asked questions about the guests. I talked about things I'm interested in. I asked people if they were interested as well. I behaved like I was a good host.

Everyone grew to be comfortable, especially me. I was comfortable joking around, being serious, and in general, just having a really good time with everyone. I engaged with everyone all day long and later into the evening as guests were heading home. I did a great job saying goodbye to each family as they departed as if it was my home, and these were my guests who I'd known for a very long time.

Eventually, everyone else was gone, and we were there with my wife's friend and her husband. At that point, we had had such a good time, and they were enjoying us so much that the husband invited me to go on a late-night fishing trip on the river. We got everything ready, packed up his boat, and drove down to the river to launch the boat. It was an amazing time on the river. We caught loads of fish, and I believe it was between 11 o'clock and midnight when we arrived back at his house. We cleaned the fish and began to fry them up. We had a great time eating great food, and in the end, the couple thanked us intensely for coming over, and the husband was extremely pleased to have finally met me.

I have to say that because of my announced change in attitude (to be the life of the party), everything was different, and everyone loved me at the end of the day. Truthfully, I really didn't do anything special other than decide not to be passive and disengaged the whole day.

I have had many other experiences like this over the years, and it always works for me to say to myself beforehand, "Act this way" or "Be this way," whatever lines up with the purpose of the speech and allows me to be comfortable with myself and my audience. My goal is to **be engaged and genuine** with my audience.

Once you have commanded fear to depart, eliminated all your preconceived ideas, and given yourself license to be the life of the party, your style can be easily discovered. Your ability to be comfortable with yourself will manifest when you are capable of standing in your power and authority.

Chapter 7 Fear Targets Power & Authority

Power & Authority

Fear directly targets and destroys power, *your power.* Oh, wait! You didn't know that you had power? *You are a public-speaking powerhouse!* Didn't you know that? Listen, when you arrive in front of an audience, whether it's on a stage, in the front of the room, or outside in front of a crowd of people, you're the man! You have the floor. So why wouldn't you think you have power?

Let's be specific here about power and authority by providing a definition for each:

Power is the ability to act or produce an effect combined with the legal or official authority, capacity, or right to possession of control or influence over others.

Authority is the granted freedom of power to influence, or command thought, opinion, or behavior.

Merely attending a meeting is the granted authority to exercise your power in that meeting. This is quickly demonstrated in the statement, "The floor is yours." The authority to exercise your power is granted, and you must choose what to do with it.

Don't miss this

The understanding of the implications of the above-clarified definitions is critical to your achievements in your presentations. You must use it. Very much like workout equipment, power exists whether we exercise it or not. You select when and where to use your power. **Fear does his best to influence your selection.** You are in control whether you realize it or not. Do you ever wonder why some people seem to command the room when they arrive at an event? They are standing in their power.

You need to understand that you have the capability to stand in your power. Your power is so strong that you can change everyone's mind. You can bring clarity and truth to your audience. You can convince them of anything. Understand that you can capture your audience and keep them engaged when you stand in your power.

You have the floor. It's the same as wearing a policeman's badge. That badge or, in this case, you having the floor *is* your authority. You have authority, and you're not even using it.

Most people not only don't realize that they have any power and authority, but by default, they give it away before they ever get close to an audience. Now that you know that you have power and authority, you need to know how to use it.

Know what to look for in the audience to confirm that you have power.

Moment of Truth

While performing the duties of the Commandant of ALS, I made an astounding discovery. I had a moment of clarity like no other. Like a whirlwind, I was overwhelmed in my mind. It was like a bomb had gone off, changing the landscape as far as the eye could see. It was a typical day on the job and then that young lady from San Antonio, Texas asked me about the key to public speaking. Suddenly, I realized that for some time now, I hadn't had the slightest bit of anxiety about public speaking, and to my shock and amazement, I knew why. **I had claimed my own power and had stopped blindly handing it over to my audience.**

After that session with the audience, I sat for some time and pondered the details. How could this be? I have freedom from fear. I have my own power. Then it hit me! I had been working so hard directing schoolhouse operations: scheduling, teaching lessons, managing my instructors, mentoring my students, planning graduations, onboarding new classes, and coordinating guest speakers and class mentors that I didn't even realize that I had naturally filtered out behaviors that give my power away and adopted behaviors that helped me maintain power.

Let me explain. **Power is all about mindset.** Let's say that you must run a big meeting. You're in charge of the meeting agenda, who's in attendance, and specifically the end results. What should be on your mind? Results. In most cases, there is generally a resistance mindset. Thoughts of delay, canceling the meeting, someone relieving you of the responsibility, avoidance, regret, etc. are examples of the resistance mindset. With the latter mindset, there is no power. Your power has already been forfeited. There is no chance of winning, only stumbling through the speech until the end and getting out of there as quickly as possible.

Power Grab

Why do some speakers get an amazing response to an opening statement while others don't? One speaker walks out in front of the audience and says, "Good afternoon," and his audience enthusiastically responds, "Good afternoon!"

Why do other speakers try this and fail, "Good morning," and a small portion of the audience mumbles inaudibly with low energy and volume? The Speaker tries again, "I said good morning!", a somewhat larger portion of the audience responds, "Good morning," hesitantly in an effort not to be prodded again to respond with another good morning.

The difference is that the first speaker has power and authority and uses it correctly, and the second speaker is desperately attempting an ineffective Power Grab. The hope is that a great response from the audience will put things on track for the presentation. It's a subconscious power struggle. The speaker is unaware of the deeper reason they are attempting the (greeting and response) attention-getter. Having tried and failed is worse than not having tried at all. Next time you see someone try and fail with the greeting/response Power Grab tactic, follow the rest of their presentation closely. It will be littered with mistakes, dwindling confidence, apologies, verbal pauses, and many other gaffs. These are speakers who gave up their power before ever stepping in front of an audience.

There is a feel in a room, an auditorium, a conference space, and a meeting room. If you're going to meet with somebody, there's an atmosphere already in that space. The minute you would arrive in that space, the vibe can change positive or negative. The sensation can be, "oh, this person who just arrived has power," or "this person who just arrived is irrelevant." It could go either way. So, if you're not 100% confident and comfortable that you have power when you walk on stage don't try the Power Grab. If you want to try and grab the power from your audience, present with confidence and do it strategically.

The strategic Power Grab for someone who doesn't already stand in their power looks like this. It's what I used to do, and this is what I know and understand. It works. Are you ready? This is what you do:

Take the floor quietly. In total silence move to the spot where you want to start your speech. Without talking make eye contact with someone in the audience until they acknowledge you looking (when they are uneasy). Then, do it to the next person, do it to someone else, you do it to the entire room. Do it until you feel the power move from your audience to you. This may sound strange, but it is real, and it works. When you can acknowledge that your audience is uncomfortable you will feel the power shift. Sometimes, it takes longer than other times, but it always works.

Once the power is moved, you're free! You can roam around. You can get close. You can stay far. You can speak loud or softly. The power has left the audience and come to you. That's the Power Grab. It's all about your comfort.

Search the internet for world champion of public speaking. Watch the beginning of five to ten champion speeches and see if you can identify the speaker's silent or not-so-silent power grab. Most of them take place in the first 5 to 15 seconds. Others, take more than 30 seconds. However, had you watched these speeches before hearing about the Power Grab, you wouldn't have even noticed that they were doing it.

This works well in a classroom setting too. After returning from a restroom break, students will often be engaged in conversations with each other and not immediately turn their attention back to you. When this happens, and you're ready to get back to the lesson, quietly walk to where one of the students can see you. Without talking, make it known that you are waiting for them to focus on you. The one will always tell the other that you are waiting for them to quit talking. Sometimes, your focused attention on the students who are talking will make another student interrupt them and tell them to be quiet while gesturing toward you. This is simply you, standing in your power. No speaking is necessary.

Mistakes Will Always Happen

I never apologize for my mistakes, and neither

should you. What is a mistake? Let's define it. In public speaking, **a mistake** is an error made in the delivery of the content of the message or any behavior or statement the speaker determines to be unwanted and, thus, should never have happened during the presentation.

Apologizing for the mistake voluntarily, lets fear back into your home and hands your power back to the audience. Apologies lower confidence and derail your focus from the task of presenting a clear, concise message to your audience.

You need to know that you can deliver the same speech a hundred times and never hear the same words come out of your mouth twice. You are going to reorganize, skip, add, and rephrase in general. The key is to be so comfortable with whatever comes out of your mouth that it doesn't startle you. It cannot have a negative effect on you. If you allow it to effect you negatively, it will become a distraction and you will most likely make an apology for it amplifying the distraction.

I can't tell you how many times I've watched a presenter say a word wrong, miss something they wanted to say, or catch themselves talking about something that isn't part of their speech and the second they notice that mistake, the speech train derails creating a pile up of massive mistakes, apologies, and embarrassing snafus.

Don't let this happen to you. Put measures in place to keep you from being shocked and feeling obligated to justify everything to your audience. Remember, they should be adjusting to you, not the other way around.

Subject Matter Expert (SME)

The best way to effectively stand in your power, strike a huge blow to fear, and keep him away is by achieving mastery of the subject matter. If you are the SME, you have essentially no reason to fear.

As a public speaker, you need to be the SME. If you are not the SME on a particular subject, then you need to learn what you can about your subject and fast. Challenge what you learn by asking questions about the information and then answering those questions for yourself (do this in your own words).

The ability to field questions on the material your presenting builds confidence and competence with your subject matter and there are two primary ways to become the SME (1) to talk on a subject that you have been trained in and had practical first-hand experience with (2) research the information you'll be speaking on and drill yourself on it over and over until you've answered all your own questions about it. There is nothing worse than finding out mid-presentation that your audience knows more about your subject than you do or that you don't know enough about an idea to articulate it clearly leaving your audience with more questions than answers.

My time at BIC proves how being the SME makes you more effective and kicks fear down to a much more manageable level. Of all the lesson plans I built and delivered at BIC; the GPS lesson was the only one that I ever repeated after graduation. If you recall, at BIC, I had to rebuild the lesson from scratch the way I wanted to teach it. The process was transformative for me. It gave me more power, authority, and control than I knew I could possess. I took an original lesson plan and a fresh new Word document and transcribed that old information over to it. As I put together each MP, I also created specific things I wanted to share that related to that point. I rewrote the transitions to fit the way I might speak a transition. When dealing with specific points I knew very little about, I transcribed them over to my new lesson plan, and I also did research on those things. I asked questions about them. I searched the internet for more information, so I'd know more than just what was in the original lesson plan. It helped me to add emphasis on those points, to understand and believe those points more than just regurgitate information.

The overall process helped me to personalize the delivery of that GPS lesson. It instilled confidence in me to be the SME when delivering that lesson. It was, for me, a new beginning as a public speaker/instructor and a catalyst driving my growth. It helped me to sharpen my abilities and gave me the power to be unique in my own way for that specific lesson. Anytime you can start from scratch and build your speech or presentation in that way, you should put in the effort. Challenge what you know. Challenge the given information. By personalizing it and adding your own stories and connections that make sense for you and for anyone else, it becomes yours from beginning to end. It ultimately empowers you to be the best you can be for that speech.

Get Saturated with Your Subject

Being the SME is accomplished when you're saturated with your subject. If you're subject is something that you're very involved with, it's automatic. For instance, ask a dedicated college football fan, "What are the three things they love most about college football?" They might have the most informative response because, naturally, they are the SME on that information. They would just need to put in some effort to organize their thoughts and deliver the information in a structured flow. Who better to talk about these details with more enthusiasm and be able to articulate the thoughts about the love of college football?

What if your boss asks you to fill in for him at an important meeting with your company's leadership and talk about the three biggest challenges your section is facing meeting the company's quarterly goals? How do you become familiar enough to be the SME, have enthusiasm about the topic, and communicate in a very articulate way? You must get saturated. You must gather as much information as you can. If there's already an outline of the details that need to be talked about, study the outline. If there are already presentation slides or other visual aids, study them and be ready to use them. Identify unfamiliar information and ask questions that will help you become familiar. One of the worst things you can do is start engaging with your audience without being properly prepared.

Not knowing the details of the subject, not being familiar with the visual aids you use, and not having enthusiasm due to lack of familiarity are all disastrous to your presentation and your credibility.

Presenting while unprepared produces a very critical

situation. At this point, oversights and gaffes start to happen. While your guard is down, fear has an opportunity to slip into the mix, elevate your heart rate, dehydrate you, and make you uber-critical of everything that you're doing and saying. Being unprepared (not the SME) weakens your armor leaving a strategic opportunity for fear to exploit your defenses and destroy your reputation, your speech, the overall presentation, and take away your true personality and confidence (your power and authority). Experiences like this, especially if they're repeated, can cause your resistance to skyrocket, making future presentations even more difficult.

Information Management

While mastering your subject and preparing your speech, you need to be looking for key elements. The most important ideas need to be labeled as main points (MPs). The details of those MPs need to be labeled subpoints (SPs).

MP: Most important ideas

SP: Supporting ideas

Your speech needs to present the information with clarity in a well-established format:

(1) Tell them what you're going to tell them. Use

an introduction and a good overview before you transition into your MP 1.

(2) Tell them. Your MPs should provide the details of what you're there to tell them with good solid transitions between each MP. Include a common thread from the beginning to the end to hold the entire speech together. (Make it make sense.)

(3) Tell them what you told them. At the end of your speech, include a summarized statement of your MPs very similar to the introductory overview. Then, end with a good closing statement that expresses completion of the subject.

When you're the SME, and you've done the work to format your message in a solid structure that lends to audience engagement, then you're ready to stand in your power.

Let's say that your presentation is a newcomer's presentation for people that were just hired. Think about and write down newcomer requirements, questions they may have as a new person, HR rules and violations, company policy, hours of operation, vacation days, and how processes work that the new worker may be unfamiliar with. Use applicable company literature. Now that you've written all your topics down, organize them into a timeline or flow so that one leads into the next. Format it so that from the beginning of your orientation to the end, it's structured. Now that you've outlined the order of things that you want to present to your newcomer, you can start drilling down your SPs so that you make sure you cover the details. Again, you want to keep a good introduction and opening overview, solid transitions between each MP and after your last MP going into your summary at the end, and then a good closure inviting and welcoming the newcomer to the team. The flow of information needs to make sense to the newcomer, or they may lose interest and miss out on some of the more important details and wasting your time and theirs.

Freedom

You know you've reclaimed the power or that your Power Grab was successful when you've said to fear, "you're no longer my fear. I don't own you anymore. You are not part of me. You are an intruder and must vacate. You have no power here. You have no authority here. Once fear is not welcome, it's all about making you legitimately and undeniably comfortable with your audience.

The way that you'll know when the power has left the audience and come back to you is to experience complete freedom when you are giving a presentation. The stage is yours. It's not your audience's stage. It's your stage. What that means is you are free to do whatever comes to your mind, whatever you want. You are free to say what you want. You are free to move around where you want.

Be sure to use your freedom strategically. Say the strategic things. Move strategically around the room. Use your hands strategically. Use your eyes strategically when you are making a point. Focus on one or two people in your audience, wherever it strategically makes sense or feels right. When that point is completed, switch your stance, move your eyes, or go to another space in the room, let it flow naturally. Focus on one or two or a small group of others, use hand gestures, and make eye contact with them. They might be, for this moment, the only subjects of this point, so talk with them in your power and freedom as if they're the only ones. You can gesture and look at other people, but they're the focus for right now.

Use your power and authority strategically. When the next point is complete, give a solid transition with that common thread that ties everything together and adds value to your presentation as you move around the room. Then focus on another person or group of people to start your next

MP.

When you can move around the room, use your hands, your eyes, your body, and your voice in a strategic way, and you know you have the freedom to do it any way that you like, *then* you know your Power Grab is successful.

You are now standing and operating in the power that is inherently yours. Now you are free to do so. Hallelujah!

Fear of Silence

Another highly important clue to know when you have successfully grabbed the power back is that you can take a break, get your mind together, formulate the words for the next point, and do it in complete silence. Your audience doesn't need to know that you're struggling to think of the next point. Your audience doesn't need to hear any kind of verbal pauses. Your audience doesn't want to see you fidgeting. Your audience may become disturbed by these things (distracted). When you are operating in your power, and you can do it in silence, it will draw more power to you because you have the confidence to stand silently in front of your audience. Your audience will respect you for it.

The longer you stand in silence, the more attention becomes focused on you, which is exactly where you want it. When your audience is distracted, side conversations begin, cell phones come out, and other things start to happen amid your presentation when your audience isn't focused on you. If that's happening, it's a clear sign that your audience has not released the power back to you.

Part III Golden Nuggets of Public Speaking

C h a p t e r   8   T r a n s i t i o n s

Transition Power

Transitions add power and fluidity to your speech. They build your credibility and keep you from stumbling over the gap between MPs. Transitions are mostly overlooked, especially in the preparation phase of putting together the presentation itself. They are also the most valuable parts of the speech. When performed correctly, they make a speech shine and keep the flow for the speaker and the audience. Transitions can enhance or destroy your flow and engage your audience or leave them behind.

Transitions are like keys. They unlock doors between one subject and another while keeping the path from beginning to end open and clear. "Road Guards out!"

I hear bad transitions all the time. Generally, the bad transition isn't a transition at all; it's a jump. A transition is a bridge between two separate ideas and, therefore, must link to two ideas somehow. Without the bridge, one must jump from point to point.

Examples of bad transitions:

With that said…

That said…

Moving on…

Now let's look at…

So much for X. What about Y?

Let's switch now to…

Looking ahead…

None of these are transitions because they don't bridge the gap between the two ideas. If they do anything, they separate or disconnect the two ideas.

A transition is only one or two sentences and should do three things (restate something from last point, relate it to the next point, and introduce the next point). They should look like this:

Example Transition:

MP 1 comes after the introduction and overview of a speech, and it must lead somewhere. That place, naturally, is MP 2.

Transition breakdown:

Restate: MP 1 comes after the introduction and overview of a speech,

Relate: and it must lead somewhere. That place,

naturally, is

Introduce: MP 2

Common Thread - Get Polished

I have developed my own structure for transitions and upgraded the classic model with two new elements. (Summarizing the first MP and linking the bridge to both MPs while including a common thread. If you want to make, your transitions truly shine, use my model, and polish your transitions until they shine.

My transitions include these three parts:

Summarize:

Summarizing surpasses simply mentioning a piece of the information from the previous MP.

Link:

The goal of a link is not only to build that bridge between MPs but to tie in a common thread from the beginning to the end of your speech. This link should also give a sense of why it's important to mention both points. It should add value.

Announce:

With the flow of information being linked, it is time to announce the arrival of the next MP.

Summarize, Link, Announce (SLA) Transition example:

MP 1: Publishing eBooks on your own is difficult, and publishing print books is much more complicated.

Transition: Knowing the difficulty of publishing eBooks, printed books being progressively more difficult and the fact that you are looking for quality in both, I strongly recommend getting help to accomplish the publishing.

MP 2: There are a lot of excellent resources to help you with publishing. Many of them can easily be found online.

Transition breakdown:

Summarize:

Knowing the difficulty of publishing eBooks, printed books being progressively more difficult

Link:

and the fact that you want to do both,

Announce:

I strongly recommend getting help to accomplish the publishing.

Common thread (which is part of Link):

Desire for quality publishing

Use your common thread in all your transitions to hold the entire speech together.

Clean up your mess

When you must talk with an audience in a one-way communication, please clean up your mess:

- Know your purpose.
- Clearly define your key points.
- Be specific and meaningful.
- Stick to your purpose and tell your audience what your key points are and why they are "key" to your overall purpose.
- Use SLA to polish off your points with solid transitions keeping everything together.

You may have a lot to say, and *talking about your subject may excite you,* but don't ramble on with endless information that may not be key to your overall purpose. Offer to stay back for a while after your presentation to take questions. Give your expertise then. This is when your extra information can be targeted and meaningful to the person or group that wants to know more.

Chapter 9 NCOICs & Section Chiefs

Showcase your workplace

If you're a Section Chief or NCOIC (or civilian department head), be proud of your team and what they do! My Vehicle Operations and ALS teams did some of the most amazing work. I believe, for most leaders, the problem is that they're so busy doing the work that they don't pick their heads up out of the weeds long enough to see over the stalks. There are so many ways that your team contributes to the overall mission. You just need to isolate those things and learn to track them and sing praises about those accomplishments. Sing the song of your team to any and everyone who stops by. Your team will love you for it.

Tips for the NCOIC or Section Chief

(prepare beforehand)

When a special guest comes to tour your work center, be prepared to showcase your workplace. Follow these eight steps to sing praises about your team every time you have a visitor:

(1) Take time and review what it is your work center

does. List out major tasks and anything extremely unique that your shop does (think seasonal and upcoming tasks as well as one-time or constant priorities).

(2) Select from that list three primary go-to discussion points that truly highlight the heart of the work your team performs. Also, note what major effects your team has on the rest of the section, unit, Group, wing, base, company, or region.

(3) Once you've narrowed down the goods. Put it into a structure that makes sense. First, an introduction of yourself and your staff is necessary (when introducing, don't make it weird). Next, put your three mission topics in an order that flows (one thing leads to the next).

(4) Be sure to highlight at least one team member's achievements. For instance, if someone has recently won an award, mention it when you introduce that team member. If someone has been instrumental in accomplishing one of your work centers' major tasks, mention the team member while discussing that topic. **Give credit and show ownership.**

(5) Add a closing statement that lends completeness and suggests to your visitor that you are done. Example: "That's a good summary of our mission, sir. Do you have any questions for myself or my team?"

(6) Keep it short, simple, and precise. This briefing should only take a minute or two, but don't be alarmed if your visitor drags it out by asking questions. Just be ready to discuss your talking points (be flexible). If the talk goes long on account of the visitor, you're good. If the talk goes long because of you, you'll need to shorten what you say. (In the case that you are the reason it goes long, ask your team for suggestions and feedback on how you can make it shorter next time. They'll love that you asked for their input!)

(7) In many cases, there will also be other work center's NCOICs present to meet and greet the visitor. Be prepared to pass the visitor on to the next work center by introducing them yourself if your commander or his rep doesn't step right in and do it themselves. Example: "That's a good summary of our mission, sir. Do you have any questions for myself or my team?" "Ok, let me introduce you to Technical Sergeant Roberts. He's the NCOIC of Vehicle Maintenance."

(8) If you're a Moses and speaking isn't for you, find an Aaron (the one who speaks well in public), sit down with him, and rehearse, rehearse, rehearse. Nevertheless, you need to go through your visitor brief several times yourself to hear what it sounds like and make the appropriate

adjustments before the next visit.

I have full confidence in you. We don't put you in that position because you *can't*. We put you in that position to see all you *can* accomplish! So, do the work up front; identify your purpose, define your audience, and keep MPs and SPs relevant to your purpose.

Life's a Speech - The Impromptu

For nearly two years, I was a Community Manager for RV resorts and Manufactured Housing communities. On one occasion, I was informed the Senior Vice President (SVP) of the company was coming to visit my community.

For the next four days, I worked on items around my community that my Regional Vice President (RVP) and I agreed needed to be addressed before the visit. My team and I worked long hours each of those days. The day before the meeting, I left work at closing time. I spent some quality time with my family then, at roughly 8:30 pm, I went back to work. I worked through the last-minute details for the meeting the next day. I departed the office just after midnight.

There were a couple of items that I needed to address before the meeting. So, I woke up early the next morning. I was exhausted and had to force myself to get up, take care of my morning chores, and make my way to the office.

I arrived about 30 minutes early with a massive headache, possibly from dehydration. A member of my team asked me a question, and as I spoke for the first time that day, my voice was so groggy it shocked both of us.

When my boss, his boss, and the SVP arrived, my headache and I were ready. After a brief handshake (fist bump) and greeting each of my bosses, we all sat down in my office to go over the details of my business. Since this was my first meeting with my SVP, he asked me to introduce myself and talk a little bit about my background.

Now the purpose of this impromptu was simply to deliver information. The distribution of the details was only subject to how I organized my thoughts. I spoke with no consideration of time. I just said what felt comfortable and, on a topic, while keeping myself from being long-winded and left it at that. It seemed to suffice.

For this impromptu, I explained:

(MP1) Where I was from originally

(MP2) A brief summary of my military career

(MP3) How long I've been working with this company

(MP4) The different jobs I've performed within the company

I had spent the greater part of the week preparing for this meeting, but I wasn't ready to talk about myself in a completely unprepared impromptu speech. I had a slow start because of my lack of rest, the headache, and the surprise of the requested introduction speech. I was struggling a bit to create a flow and keep the verbal pauses to a minimum. After about 30 seconds, I recognized those verbal pauses and responded accordingly. I considered my audience, decided what information I wanted to include from that point on, and picked up the pace. I quickly settled into a rhythm, transitioned from one MP to another, and eliminated my verbal pauses altogether. I traversed through the rest of my topic somewhat effortlessly (approximately 5-6 minutes).

There are times, while in the middle of a speech, that you may have to adjust everything. In this case, don't freak out, and don't telegraph your struggle to your audience. You will serve yourself well if you just **breathe, slow down**, and **concentrate on exactly what you want to deliver to your audience**.

Slow is Smooth and Smooth is Fast

I was told while attending the Anti-Terrorism

Evasive Driving Course, regarding racing, "slow is smooth and smooth is fast." This holds true in racing, and it certainly holds true in public speaking. If you slow down, you'll give your mind a chance to adapt to the speech. You'll "click" into gear, which will bring confidence and clarity as you proceed, and then you'll be capable of naturally speeding up to what your mind can handle without errors. This is usually just the kind of pace your audience needs (*All-natural, genuine speech*).

Chapter 10 Audience Engagement

What Turns an Audience Off also Destroys your Credibility

"Bear with me. I know this subject is boring,

but we must get through it."

-Any Random Speaker

Have you ever watched a speech, and somehow the speaker just turned you off? Have you had that experience where it's very difficult for you to pay attention and engage with the content?

This is just to give you some ideas of behaviors that you should avoid and some you should be sure to do to keep from losing your audience and your credibility over minute details that have a significant impact on your audience's attention span (This list is not all-inclusive).

Nervous Chatter

As a speaker, sometimes the pressure to perform causes you to say things that you are thinking that you never should say out loud with your audience. For instance, self-talk, "Oh, I shouldn't have done that." "Let me turn this this way. Then we can get started." "That's not frustrating." These statements don't pertain to the overall topic or purpose of your speech. They are for your mind to think and not for your mouth to say. Audiences don't like nervous chatter. It tears down your credibility.

Off-Topic

Another way to lose your audience quickly is by drifting off-topic. If you've been clear from the beginning, "Hey guys, my name is Wade. I'm here to talk to you today about MP1, MP2, and MP3. Let's get into it." Your audience will immediately identify when you've gone off-topic. While talking about MP1, you may drift off topic like this, "That reminds me of a family story. Let me tell you, my father…" telling a story about your father has no relevance to your topic. The longer you talk about your father and do not stick to the MP, the more you will lose your audience. To give a quote from your father is one thing, "My father used to say…" say the quote and then get back to the topic. Whatever you include that might seem off-topic needs to be relevant, and you need to transition right back to your topic. That's beautiful. But, if you linger on an off-topic subject with some long-winded story that isn't automatically relevant and immediately transitions back to the topic, you will throw your audience fast. They'll stop listening. They'll start fidgeting. They may even start side conversations because you're just too long-winded and off-topic with illustrations or side stories.

Visual Aids

The same thing goes for the use of visual aids. You want to make sure that the use of visual aids does not become a distraction. To get in the weeds about how a chart is put together or talking about something other than the visual aid you're showing your audience becomes irrelevant. This is a time waster and a huge distraction for your audience. If you have important information to share that isn't represented on your visual aid, take it down until you need it again. This will keep your audience's mind on what you're saying and not what you're displaying.

If you're going to use illustrations, stories, metaphors, and/or visual aids, make sure that they are relevant. Measure their value and if there is no real value added to the topic, don't use them, or briefly mention them for content's sake, but don't stick with it. Don't make it the focal point because it is naturally irrelevant.

To save on your credibility, make sure that any handouts or other visual aids are clean, legible, up to date, relevant. It deletes credibility when your audience identifies flaws in your visual aids, and it usually doesn't take much effort to recreate the aids in good condition. This is an easy fix.

Technical Difficulty

Something that turns off your audience right away and immediately surrenders your power back to them is not having done a complete check beforehand of the auditorium, the sound equipment, your slides, the computer, or if it's an online meeting, making sure that your connection is good, and all the meeting invites were sent out properly. The last thing your audience wants to do is sit through you, trying to work on technical difficulties or waiting for other members to log in online. People don't want to see you fumbling with your whiteboard, slides, computer, or microphone. No one wants to sit and watch your antivirus go through a system check because you haven't used that computer in weeks nor waiting for your computer to restart to install updates. Your credibility can be completely wrecked while you wait for the computer issue that you should have taken care of well beforehand (preferably the day before).

Apologetic Behavior

A terribly distracting behavior is offering apologies.

Of course, you're going to be the first one to recognize that you've made a mistake or error. Don't bring attention to it. Your audience may not have noticed. Do whatever you have to do, tell yourself whatever you must tell yourself, but whatever you do, don't apologize.

Apologizing to your audience when you make a mistake takes away from the purpose of the speech, gives fear a chance to take over your presentation, and ensures the power rests with your audience.

Once you've recognized a mistake, quickly determine if correcting it is necessary or not (make that decision instantly). If no correction is necessary, simply continue with your presentation.

If the mistake makes you inaccurate, restate it correctly, but don't apologize for the mistake. Just fix it and move on. Handling it in this way makes you credible and says to your audience, "I'm in charge and can handle whatever happens." The moment you start apologizing to your audience, you are saying to them: "I have no power. You have no reason to listen to me. I don't have any authority. I'm irrelevant. You are way more important than I am. So, just go ahead and ignore everything else I have to say."

Do not apologize for any errors or mistakes. Do not apologize if you're computer goes down or you have some other technical difficulty. Work through it. If you need to give your audience a break, do it with confidence. Release them of the responsibility of paying attention to you and then get back to them, bringing them back together when everything's corrected. Then, you can press on with your speech, but don't make it a huge apology session. If you've already said, "Oh, I'm sorry, guys, bear with me here. I'll get this squared away, and we can get back to the presentation" do not say it again. Do not apologize profusely. There is no need. It just becomes another turn off for your audience.

Announcing Bad News

"OK, guys, I know this briefing is boring, so bear with me. We must get through it." Don't make a negative announcement about your content. You're turning your audience off without them even having a say. Your audience will think to themselves, "Well, if this is going to be boring, I might as well think about the vacation I have planned." "What am I going to do Friday night because..." "Well, lunch sure is sounding good right now." So, whatever you do never, *never* make a negative comment about your content. Just don't do it. You're giving your audience license to change the channel, tune you out, and do something else the whole time you're talking.

You *must* stop telling yourself negative ideas about your content. Your content needs to make you excited. If it doesn't excite you, it's you own fault. You must put in the effort and discover how to talk your content in a way that keeps you excited. When you are excited about your speech the audience will be excited too.

Surprise Failure

No matter how good the idea seems, don't play the surprise game with your audience. What you plan on doing and the clarity of your overall purpose is extremely critical to a successful speech. You don't want to jeopardize that in any way.

You need to be clear about your intention from the very beginning of your speech. Audiences do not want to try and figure out where you're going while you're talking. Audiences appreciate being able to truly lock in on the purpose being introduced and sticking to it from the beginning to the end. Audiences do not like surprises. Audiences *do not* like surprises.

If the presentation is to answer a question, then the answer can be revealed at any moment successfully because your presentation will build on the question to set up the answer. The purpose, in this case, is to provide the audience with the answer.

However, don't deliver a standard message with the intention of making part of it a surprise. Holding back information from your audience on purpose until the moment you feel like surprising them is never good. It deprives the audience of the key element that they need to maintain engagement with your presentation. They may not know that you're holding back information, but they will sense something is off, and the minute they do, they will lose interest, or their mind will become preoccupied with trying to learn or figure out what it is you're withholding. At that point, they won't be listening intently to what you're saying.

When you decide to spring your surprise, it will be like having your audience going full steam ahead on one track, and suddenly, the audience is being jerked in a new direction to another line of thinking, something they were not expecting.

Movies can sometimes get away with a surprise because it's a story. To have a storyline jerk to a new direction like that is different for a movie audience. It's part of the filmmaking, storytelling kind of thing, but audiences aren't ready for that kind of drama to take place during a speech. That is not how they take in the information. That's not how they engage with you. They're mentally following along in a different way. So, surprises in general, are not good. It's a simple way to lose your audience and lower your credibility.

Here's a personal observation from my time as the ALS Commandant. The Air Force story speech that we have our students perform includes in MP3 a talk on whether the student plans on staying in the Air Force or separating. Roughly 25 percent of the students decide to present the speech while keeping it a secret as to whether they're going to reenlist or separate all the way up until they reach MP3 in the speech.

Every time I have witnessed a student try to keep it a secret until they get to MP3, it has gone wrong. It lost the audience. It makes it harder for the presenter to keep things straight because they are putting energy and effort into keeping this secret and they are expecting some kind of audience reaction.

The flow is already obstructed because they're holding back. There may be a way to deliver, and have it been a complete and total surprise, but at the same time, the shock significance, the overall value that you would get from that information being revealed, isn't spectacular. At this point, your audience has heard your story. They've heard about what you did before the Air Force, they've heard about what you do in the Air Force, and now you're just saying, I'm going to stick this out and continue with my career. I have a few more goals I want to meet. Or you're saying, I'm ready to separate. I want to go back to college or whatever the other pathway is.

So, to hold that back as some kind of ultimate surprise that's going to win over your audience isn't going to have that effect at all. This little piece of information isn't going to boost your speech performance. Surprises, in general, are not good. There are many other times I have witnessed a person trying to hold back and wait for a moment of surprise during a speech, and it just doesn't add value as one would think.

Think of it this way. In everyday life, you might decide to keep something a secret while working on getting someone's participation. Then, that person confronts you, "Why are you lying to me?" "I'm not lying to you." "You didn't tell me about this. Why didn't you tell me about this?" "I don't know. I guess I thought it would be funny to have it be a surprise." "Well, it isn't funny. I don't appreciate it at all. You should have just told me at the beginning."

My suggestion is to keep the information flowing freely and clearly for your audience. They always want to know where you are and where you're going. No surprises.

Plowing Snow

Another thing speakers do when they're withholding information is make statements along the way like, "I'll tell you about that in a minute" or "I'll cover this more in MP3". Audiences don't like to be put off. It reminds me of plowing snow. Your goal is to get the snow from one end of the parking lot to the other, but you're just pushing the snow off to the side. Then, you must come back and push it off to the side again, then come back again and again. Eventually, you'll get all that original snow from one end of the parking lot to the other, but it takes time, energy, and special maneuvering, and the snow is just stalled along the way.

Think of your presentation this way. Just carry the snow and walk it down to the end of the parking lot. We're starting at the beginning. We're going all the way through to the other end with no halts, no interruptions, no surprises, and no waiting periods where the audience doesn't know what's happening. Everything flows extremely well. Take your idea from the beginning to the end and don't circle back and circle back and keep pushing off that secret until the end.

Hallway conversations

When I think about public speaking, I imagine a speech or presentation taking place just like a random conversation in a hallway. Have you ever had someone stop you in the hallway and ask you a question? How did you respond? Was it stressful? Were afraid?

Think about every speech or presentation as just another encounter with someone or some group, the same way you would stop in a hallway and greet them. Maybe talk to them about the weather or sports. There are no nerves in the hallway. There is no risk in the hallway. Your audience doesn't have any power over you in the hallway. It's just you and them, just you and your audience. It's precisely the same during your official presentation.

You and I should be able to speak with a large audience as if we just met each other in a hallway and sparked up a conversation, but somehow there's fear related to speaking to an audience. This fear can sneak up on you, overwhelm you and disable your ability to maintain a decent flow in a speech, even just to be able to communicate your message clearly. You will need to address some of your personal thoughts to change your public speaking performance to be more natural and comfortable, like a hallway conversation. This may take some practice, but it can easily be done.

Sales Position

Sometimes your presentation is not one-way communication. Your presentation may be a scripted dialogue between you and your audience. For instance, if you're in sales, you need to have product knowledge so that when you're with your customer talking about your product and they have a question, you'll be able to field that question with the right information. Because you have product knowledge, you're the SME. However, you also need to be ready to present the scripted MPs in your presentation.

You'll know the power is yours and that you're standing in your power when you can demonstrate the ability to stay on track when a question is asked that requires extra thinking on your part, something not naturally part of your given presentation to sell your product. You should be able to comfortably go silent and, without an outline, be able to get back to where you left off in the sales presentation.

Many salespeople fail to get to the end of their sales presentation and ask for the customer's business without getting caught up during that natural dialog with the customer and losing track of the details they were supposed to ensure were presented the customer.

Every buyer needs to be informed. They need to have all the information available to make a legitimate informed decision. When a salesperson gets lost in the customer's dialog, they lose track of their own presentation and therefore lose the audience engagement that it takes to secure the sale.

Adding Enthusiasm

If you have little to no desire to talk on a subject, by default, your performance will be subpar at best. You'll have to do something to keep your interest during the speech to keep your audience truly engaged. Enthusiasm is the key. When you are enthusiastic, your audience will be too.

On occasion, you may have to present a topic that doesn't interest you. If so, it's your job to present this information, and my suggestion is to find something somewhere that *does* interest you and weave it in in a way that relates it to the information you must deliver. This could come in the form of jokes, personal stories, external stories, nicknames for ideas or people in your speech, or associations you create as the speaker.

Let's say that you have a safety subject to talk about, and you think that subject is irrelevant and, in general, you just don't care. There's a way to take something that you *are* interested in and include it in your discussion about safety to make the speech more interesting to you. Add something you've been through, people that you know who have had a safety incident, or you can find a link in something else that's not safety-related whatsoever. Either way, link one or more of your interests to your safety discussion.

You may choose to link the game of basketball, a certain player, or a certain team with the MPs of the safety speech. You can do this quite easily if you take some time. Think of football, basketball, or anything that's commonly known that your audience would automatically relate to, even if they're not as enthusiastic about it as you. This will bring your level of enthusiasm for your speech to the point where people will listen to you talk about safety, not because safety just got cooler, but because it created enthusiasm in you. It gives you another way to stand in your power and keep your audience engaged.

If you're adding something to your presentation that you're passionate about, an easy way to introduce that idea is to use it as the common thread throughout your entire presentation. Use it as the one thing that links everything together.

Maybe you want to tell a parallel story about a specific game while talking about safety. Your audience will be listening to two parallel ideas, safety and how it relates to a game. When you move between MPs, you shift the safety-related idea, as well as the game. So, in the end, you have a game as a common thread creating value and adding to the overall enthusiasm of the speech.

Get creative with your speech. Speeches do not have to be specifically and only about the subject matter. If you're excited about your team, add your team to your presentation. If you're excited about golf, use that. If you're an avid book reader, use a popular book that you've read and weave that into your presentation. Find ways to add pieces of information, stories, or related items that add extra value to give you and your audience an emotional link and enthusiasm.

If you're standing there speaking as if reading from a textbook and you don't add anything to make you the enthusiastic expert, you're going to lose your audience and your credibility will suffer. When you lose your audience, the visible feedback they give you will cause you to stumble. When you realize they're busy with other things and their attention isn't on you anymore, fear will strike. Anxiety, fidgeting, and less eye contact will diminish and derail your enthusiasm and your presentation.

What if you have a 4-hour presentation? You've got to take restroom and lunch breaks. Things that you can use as a common thread or add value, humor, and enthusiasm to your speech are things that you've picked up from your audience during the first, second, or third hour. Incorporate those things again when you come back from a break. Do a summary of what you covered the previous hour, including some of the things that your audience said or questions that they asked during the break, and re-answer them.

Grab whatever you can grab from the previous hour and throw it back in with an audience to keep them engaged and the enthusiasm high. It's going to keep you in a good mood. It's going to bring more power to what you're doing and to you as a speaker.

Your audience will appreciate you restating something that happened to them. You become closer and more comfortable with each other the more times you can joke about something someone said, things that weren't accurate, or anything that you can find that adds humor, grab it, reuse it, and throw it in again. Your audience will reveal to you visually and maybe even verbally if something has been overused. Keep that in mind as well.

What's your Banana?

There's a scene in an old comedy called Naked Gun. In this movie, Al is too tall for the camera to see his face. Frank (Al's police partner) and Al are talking with another person. "There is something on the side of your mouth Al." Frank says. Al reaches out of the movie frame to wipe something off his face. "No, no, no, the other side." Then Al wipes the other side of his face, and half a banana falls on the desk. This is the ridiculous comedy that I think best describes continued blunders as a public speaker.

I use this movie moment to express concerns the audience can clearly observe that the speaker may be oblivious to. Therefore, good feedback is like someone pointing out what banana you have on your face. Every speaker should strive to determine their banana(s). Your banana may be the one thing that keeps audiences from connecting with you and your subject. Nerves and the challenge of delivering a flawless speech can make it hard for a speaker to acknowledge all their own quirks or mishaps they may have. Every time you eliminate a banana, you grow your audience's engagement. Get excited, grow yourself, and be genuine.

T h a n k   Y o u

Thanks for reading! Please add a short review on Amazon.com or Goodreads.com and let me know what you think! Every book review counts, and every book sold contributes to the overall goal of delivering people from fear and helping them stand in their power.

For further information, a free public speaking consultation, join the community or sign up in the Dojo for an exhilarating training experience, please visit:

www.MyPremierTraining.com

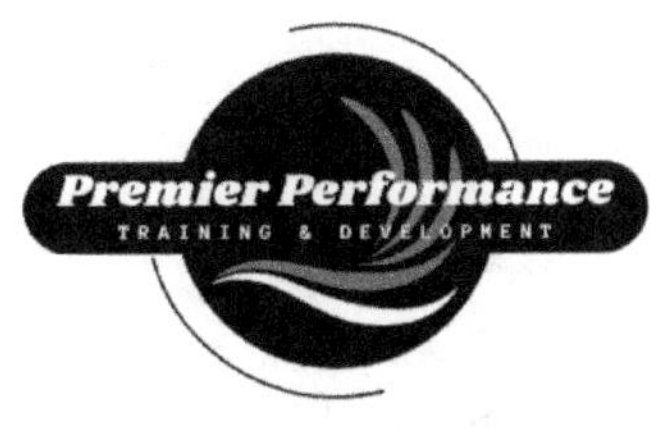

When you join the community, you'll find free resources, blog articles, videos, training materials, handouts (as they become available), and a community of people working to achieve similar goals. The Fear Driven Speech community is a place to grow together, one speech at a time.

Thanks, and may God be with you in your journey to

fearless speech delivery!

A u t h o r   B i o

Master Sergeant Carter has been a trainer since 1998 and became a Community College of the Air Force Instructor in 2006 when he joined the instructor cadre at the Vehicle Operations Apprentice Course at Fort Leonard Wood, MO. He has experience in multiple public speaking environments and with audiences up to 600 people. Sergeant Carter's emotional intelligence it's extremely high, and his ability to highlight and explain a concept or principle is superb.

Sergeant Carter has held management positions with several different companies, but he has always been an investor in people. His books, his business and his life are just that, an investment in people.

Sergeant Carter is genuine and has a passion for people where others don't. What people find most fascinating about Sergeant Carter is his ability to lead, allowing his teams to create solutions and perform at their highest levels through empowerment, coaching, and care.

Sergeant Carter has held several sales positions in which his customers were blown away by his personality and his ability to connect with them and create solutions that matter rather than just make a sale and earn a dollar. Sergeant Carter has an unorthodox approach that works. Since leaving the Air Force, Sergeant Carter has not lost his passion for mentoring and coaching others.

Leave a book review on Amazon.com or Goodreads.com and connect with and follow Sergeant Carter at:

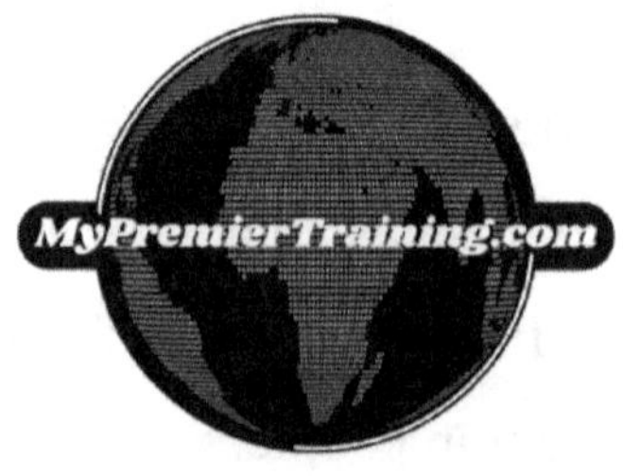

www.ingramcontent.com/pod-product-compliance
Lightning Source LLC
Chambersburg PA
CBHW052018150726
47999CB00004B/1708